A Personal Worship Resource
(Includes Journal, Art and Music)

Featuring the Paintings of Daniel Bonnell
Musical Arrangements by Basil Alter
with
Reflections from Various Contributing Writers

Copyright © 2021 Lana Lee Marler.

All rights reserved. No part of this book may be used or reproduced by any means, graphic, electronic, or mechanical, including photocopying, recording, taping or by any information storage retrieval system without the written permission of the author except in the case of brief quotations embodied in critical articles and reviews.

Archway Publishing books may be ordered through booksellers or by contacting:

Archway Publishing
1663 Liberty Drive
Bloomington, IN 47403
www.archwaypublishing.com
844-669-3957

Because of the dynamic nature of the Internet, any web addresses or links contained in this book may have changed since publication and may no longer be valid. The views expressed in this work are solely those of the author and do not necessarily reflect the views of the publisher, and the publisher hereby disclaims any responsibility for them.

Album Music Hyperlink https://cast.jacobsladdercdc.org/

Book Front Cover Art: *Cast Your Net* by Daniel Bonnell
Book Back Cover Art: *Stairway to Heaven* by Julie Hamilton
Title Page Art: *Yellow Orange Blue Watercolor Square design 3* by Sharon Freeman

ISBN: 978-1-6657-1236-1 (sc)

Library of Congress Control Number: 2021918995

Print information available on the last page.

Archway Publishing rev. date: 03/24/2022

All Scripture taken from the King James Version of
the Bible except where noted otherwise.

Additional sources are as follows:

Scripture quotations marked NIV are taken from the THE HOLY BIBLE, NEW INTERNATIONAL VERSION®,NIV® Copyright © 1973, 1978, 1984, 2011 by Biblica, Inc.® Used by permission. All rights reserved worldwide.

Scripture quotations marked ESV are taken from The ESV® Bible (The Holy Bible, English Standard Version®). ESV® Text Edition: 2016. Copyright © 2001 by Crossway, a publishing ministry of Good News Publishers. The ESV® text has been reproduced in cooperation with and by permission of Good News Publishers. Unauthorized reproduction of this publication is prohibited. All rights reserved.

Scripture quotations marked CSB are taken from The Christian Standard Bible. Copyright © 2017 by Holman Bible Publishers. Used by permission. Christian Standard Bible®, and CSB® are federally registered trademarks of Holman Bible Publishers, all rights reserved.

In Dedication

to

My Dear Husband,

Rev. William D. Marler,

for

His Love and Prayers,

Encouragement, Scholarly Support

and

Generosity of Spirit Contributed to this Endeavor.

A Word of Special Thanks

to

Basil Alter

and

Kathern Harless

for

Profound Expertise

and

Tireless Dedication

To this Labor of Love

For the Kingdom of God.

In Gratitude

Rev. Kenton C. Burnette, United Methodist Ordained Elder, Retired,
An Enduring Example of Spiritual Balance and Servant Leadership

Bishop Kenneth L. Carder,
Williams Distinguished Professor Emeritus, Duke Divinity School,
Unbiased Discerner of God's Word and Advocate of Truth.

The Rev. Dr. Stephen H. Cook, 2nd Baptist Church, Memphis, TN,
Pastor, Constant Friend and Spiritual Guide.

Shirley Lyles,
Gifted Writer, Educator and Servant to the Underserved

The Rev. L. Noland Pipes, Jr.,
Anglican Priest and Mentor in my adult faith journey.

Andrew L. Smith,
Religious Author, Friend and Wordsmith

Contents

Foreward..xv

Preface..xix

Introduction...xxiii

Grace Chapter with *This Little Light of Mine* by Lori Pittenger....................1

    Scripture, Prayer and Reflection..3

    Vortex of the Christ by Daniel Bonnell..4

    Grace Commentary by Lana Lee Marler..5

    Jesus Calms the Storm by Daniel Bonnell..8

    Amazing Grace by John Newton, music hyperlink..............................9

    Grace Reflections..10

Peace Chapter with *This Little Light of Mine* by Lori Pittenger..................15

    Scripture, Prayer and Reflection..17

    Touch by Jelena Jovanovic...18

    Peace Commentary by Lana Lee Marler..19

    The Right Hand of St. Francis by Daniel Bonnell.............................22

    A Quiet Room by Lana Lee Marler, music hyperlink.......................23

Peace Reflections..24

Provision Chapter with *This Little Light of Mine* by Lori Pittenger..............29

   Scripture, Prayer and Reflection..31

   Consider the Lilies by Lori Wright Mackert......................................32

   Provision Commentary by Lana Lee Marler.......................................33

   Pieta Meditation by Daniel Bonnell..36

   There is No I in You by Lana Lee Marler, music hyperlink................37

   Provision Reflections...38

Faith Chapter with *This Little Light of Mine* by Lori Pittenger..................43

   Scripture, Prayer and Reflection..45

   The Gift of Self by Maria Hunt..46

   Faith Commentary by Lana Lee Marler..47

   Jesus the Boy by Daniel Bonnell..52

   Just by unknown author and Lana Lee Marler, music hyperlink.....53

   Faith Reflections..54

Love Chapter with *This Little Light of Mine* by Lori Pittenger....................59

   Scripture, Prayer and Reflection..61

Mary Standing before Gabriel by Daniel Bonnell..................62

Love Commentary by Lana Lee Marler..................63

Jesus Wept by Daniel Bonnell..................66

From Love...To Love by Lana Lee Marler, music hyperlink..................67

Love Reflections..................68

Mercy Chapter with *This Little Light of Mine* by Lori Pittenger..................73

    Scripture, Prayer and Reflection..................75

    The Father's Forgiveness by Daniel Bonnell..................76

    Mercy Commentary by Lana Lee Marler..................77

    Glimpse of the Christ by Daniel Bonnell..................80

    His Face by H. Lemmel & Lana Lee Marler, music hyperlink..................81

    Mercy Reflections..................82

Obedience Chapter with *This Little Light of Mine* by Lori Pittenger..................87

    Scripture, Prayer and Reflection..................89

    Trinity and the Cross by Daniel Bonnell..................90

    Obedience Commentary by Lana Lee Marler..................91

    Heart and Hook by Thomas Cheatham..................96

Jesus Said adapted by Lana Lee Marler, music hyperlink.................97

Obedience Reflections..98

Hope Chapter with *This Little Light of Mine* by Lori Pittenger.................103

Scripture, Prayer and Reflection..105

Spirit of Hope by Maria Hunt..106

Hope Commentary by Lana Lee Marler..107

Hope in the Heights by Daniel Bonnell..110

Prayer of the Goat adapted by Lana Lee Marler, music hyperlink....111

Hope Reflections..112

Joy Chapter with *This Little Light of Mine* by Lori Pittenger.................117

Scripture, Prayer and Reflection..119

The Prodigal and the Father by Daniel Bonnell..120

Joy Commentary by Lana Lee Marler..121

The Road Home by Daniel Bonnell..124

Amazing Love...adapted by Lana Lee Marler, music hyperlink........125

Joy Reflections..126

Glory Chapter with *This Little Light of Mine* by Lori Pittenger.................131

  Scripture, Prayer and Reflection..133

  Vortex of the Christ by Daniel Bonnell..134

  Glory Commentary by Lana Lee Marler.....................................135

  Heaven and Earth by Daniel Holeman.......................................140

  O Holy Vision by Lana Lee Marler, music hyperlink.................141

  Glory Reflections..142

Benediction..147

Even so..149

References...151

References Editor..163

Artists..164

Featured Music Arranger and Contributing Arrangers....................170

Sound Engineers..171

Music...172

Paradox..174

About the Author...175

Album Music Hyperlink <https://cast.jacobsladdercdc.org/>

Foreward

by The Rev. Dr. Stephen H. Cook

On the heels of a years-long time of upheaval and unrest – a time that gave birth to a new republic that is still striving to live up to its highest and best ideals – Benjamin Franklin wrote to a friend in France. Included in his letter was a line that has lived on for centuries since. Franklin observed, "Our new Constitution is now established, everything seems to promise it will be durable; but, in this world, nothing is certain except death and taxes." Over the course of the year 2020 and beyond, no one has been untouched by the effects of the global health pandemic. So much of what we presumed was durable proved otherwise. Those of us who long for certainty, consistency, and predictable patterns of routine frequently found ourselves struggling to get our bearings.

In your hands you hold a gift that will help provide a steadying, strengthening force for the living of these days. *Cast Your Net Again* is an eclectic collection of scripture, prayer, music, written words, and artistic expressions that afford us gracious gifts of perspective and assurance. We hear and see the perspectives of fellow pilgrims who seek to live faithfully as followers of Christ. Likewise, by way of the wisdom gleaned from Christian traditions that span the centuries, we receive the assurance that we are not alone. So much of what we have experienced since the onset of the coronavirus pandemic has had a disorienting effect on our day-to-day lives, the institutions, and the organizations on which we have counted, and – if we are being honest – on our faith.

Lana Marler has done extraordinary work and gone to greater lengths than any of us will ever fully know to bring this book to life. Her passion and commitment to using her God-given gifts for the greater good of others comes through in every element of this work. This labor of love embodies her commitment to Christ and to living and serving in Christian community. Hers is a faith that does not exist in a vacuum. Instead, her faith has taken shape and finds its fullest expression as she lives and serves with and among others. As you and I have the opportunity to peruse these pages and linger over the images, or to let the words of ancient scripture and contemporary authors find new life in our hearts and minds, we are likely to find ourselves aware that there is more that endures beyond death and taxes. There are gifts of faith, hope, and love that sustain and keep us through it all.

As a pastor who serves one of the congregations with which Lana is connected via her vast network of relationships, I have come to count on her for a gift she gives me every seven days. This is something that happens out of the public eye in the early hours of each Sunday morning. Without fail, before gathering with the people of God for worship, she sends me a word of blessing, an offering of encouragement, and a prayer. In some sense, I feel as if this book is an expanded version of the kind of gift that she has been sharing with me (and heaven only knows how many others!) with care, compassion, and grace in every message. While old Mr. Franklin might have famously spoken to the certainty of death and taxes' durability, I feel certain that you will find the collection you are holding now will endure as a resource of inspiration, hope, and blessing for years to come.

Stephen H. Cook
Senior Pastor
Second Baptist Church
Memphis, TN

Go not, my soul, in search of Him,
Thou wilt not find Him there,
Or in the depths of shadow dim,
Or heights of upper air.

For not in far-off realms of space
The Spirit hath His throne;
In every heart He findeth place,
And waiteth to be known.

Thou shalt not want for company,
Nor pitch thy tent alone;
Th' indwelling God will go with thee,
And show thee of His own.

O gift of gifts, O grace of grace,
That God should condescend
To make thy heart His dwelling-place
And be thy daily friend!

Then go not thou in search of Him,
But to thyself repair;
Wait thou within the silence dim,
And thou shalt find Him there.

F. L. Hosmer

I am so happy that Lana has published another book. Her writings always make you pause, ponder and think. I am always brought closer to our God when I read, listen, and observe her work.

Andrew L. Smith, Author and Lay Pastor

With the assistance of God-given insights, this book provides an inspiration to a closer walk with God. Through the use of scripture, prayer, poetry, art, music, and theological insights the author has given us a resource which, if used faithfully, will deepen our relationship with the God most fully revealed in Jesus Christ.

Rev. Kenton Burnette, Retired Elder UMC

Preface

My prayer bird was cold – would not away,
Although I set it on the edge of the nest.
Then I bethought me of the story old –
Love-fact or loving fable, Thou knowest best
How, when the children had made sparrows of clay,
Thou mad'st them birds, with wings to flutter and fold:
Take, Lord, my prayer in Thy hand and make it pray.

Based on the story of the child Jesus
And the Apocryphal Gospel of Thomas

(Graciously offered by a friend...*For Such a Time as This*)
A Year of Panic or Peace

Birds never held much interest for me, not like dogs, cats, monkeys, or horses do for some people. As a child, robins' blue eggshells briefly piqued my interest in the springtime. Later, occasionally mimicking the calls of cardinals and owls, who would then answer, fascinated me. But during the pandemic, it was the birds that kept me sane.

The first week of the 2020 lockdown provided a welcome break to tackle small projects that had lingered on a to-do list. Once completed, I chafed at the restrictions. Schools and many businesses closed. Parents were laid off. Employees who remained, often caught the virulent COVID virus. Basic supplies like toilet paper, soap, and sanitizer disappeared from store shelves in a blitz. The children, who depended on free lunch and snacks at school, had none. Lacking employment and income, many parents who could barely manage expenses for rent and utilities did not have spare gasoline to pick up their children's meals every day at school. Not only that, parents instantly became teachers for their children confined at home.

Now forbidden to provide a safe haven for children after school, and with them doing online learning at home, what would fill my time? There were no lessons to plan, no snacks to buy, no time for playing basketball or swinging or being creative together. Life suddenly felt stifling.

What to do? Everyone needs to eat. My husband and I began preparing meals through the Jacob's Ladder Ministry a few days each week for children, their families, and infirm seniors. That re-established purpose and a worthy goal. Weeks led to months of semi-isolation, mask-wearing, and social distancing. Vacations were canceled. Family visits ended. Churches closed. Not everyone had enough fortitude to bear the isolation. Once-cheerful people turned sullen. The incidences of suicides, domestic violence cases, and drug-related fatal shootings skyrocketed along with the COVID deaths. Turning on the nightly news became a type of self-flagellation. Feelings escalated from annoyance to anger to rage until I stopped watching. Everyone seemed to be angry – either about what was happening or what wasn't.

The birds, though, came every day to our feeders. They were my solace and entertainment. The finches and cardinals pecked away for a few seeds. A redheaded woodpecker hung upside down so it could reach a few morsels. The hummingbirds gingerly clung with their claws as they sucked the red sugary juice. Momentarily their fluttering wings quieted. Then they would float to a nearby limb and patiently wait for their next turn. Occasionally, the hummingbirds bumped into each other when trying to land. But in late summer as they prepared to migrate, they became desperate and selfish, pushing each other, and ultimately engaging in an all-out assault on each other in the air.

Meditating while staring out the kitchen window, a familiar verse came to mind. "Look at the birds of the air; they do not sow or reap or store away in barns, and yet your heavenly Father feeds them. Are you not much more valuable than they? Who of you by worrying can add a single hour to life? Therefore do not worry about tomorrow, for tomorrow will worry about itself. Each day has trouble enough of its own." (Matthew 6:26-27,34)

Yes, clearly each day had plenty of trouble. People marched with signs, sprayed obscenities on public buildings, looted stores, threw objects at police, torched buildings, and shot bystanders. Yet, the birds did not seem to notice. They just kept doing what they always did. After all, what was the purpose of worrying? "Who of you by worrying can add a single hour to his life? Since you cannot do this very little thing, why do you worry about the rest?" (Luke 12:25-26)

Day after day messages kept appearing in my devotional readings. "Trust in the Lord with all your heart and lean not on your own understanding; in all your ways acknowledge him, and he will make your paths straight." (Proverbs 3:5-6) "There is a time for everything, and a season for every activity under heaven." (Ecclesiastes 3:1) It doesn't matter if I don't understand the meaning or don't like it. "Even to your old age and gray hairs I am he, I am he who will sustain you. I have made you and I will carry you; I will sustain you and I will rescue you." (Isaiah 46:4) "Do not be anxious about anything, but in everything by prayer and petition, with thanksgiving present your requests to God. And the peace of God which transcends all understanding, will guard your hearts and minds in Christ Jesus." (Philippians 4:6-7) And gradually, I was at peace.

Dozens of coots splashed in the lake, scrawny legs waving in the air as they dived for sustenance. The Canadian geese swam away as the coots came closer to shore. When ripe acorns were plentiful in the fall, the geese crowded the lawn searching for the best-looking plump ones. After a time, the leader would honk, and off they all would waddle, plop into the lake, and paddle away. In December the pelicans returned. They floated around like giant white cotton balls clinging close to each other. Some days an entire armada floated past, first the coots, followed by the geese, then the majestic pelicans formed the rear guard. To them the year was like any other, and they lived just as they did every year.

Shirley Lyles

Introduction

Lord...
My soul is so dry that by itself it cannot pray;
Yet you can squeeze from it the juice of a thousand prayers.
My soul is so parched that by itself it cannot love;
Yet you can draw from it boundless love for you and for my neighbour.
My soul is so cold that by itself it has no joy;
Yet you can light the fire of heavenly joy within me.
My soul is so feeble that by itself it has no faith;
Yet by your power my faith grows to a great height.
Thank you for prayer, for love, for joy, for faith;
Let me be always prayerful, loving, joyful and faithful.

Guigo the Carthusian (d.1188)

It was the Spring of 2020 when I felt compelled to begin writing this book. I had found myself in the same place spiritually as Guigo the Carthusian when he wrote this prayer at the beginning of the second millennium. It is an odd but comforting realization that the same truths offered in this prayer spanned the decades, generations and almost an entire millennia to broadcast anew from the depths of my own soul. A saying from the African American evangelist, Sojourner Truth (1797-1883) is applicable now and always, in that "Truth is power and it prevails."

It was the time of pandemic in the world and as mentioned in the Preface of this book, there was no such thing as living a normal life, nor was there hope that any concept of normalcy as we knew it would ever return. *The truth is, of course, that what one regards as interruptions are precisely one's life.* (C. S. Lewis) In spite of the daily challenges and despair over the loss of life, truth resonated from my inner-self. Ours was not the first and only generation to be confronted with a likewise catastrophic event and most probably would not be the last. The question of the response of the human spirit is paramount – particularly when one identifies his or herself as a follower of Truth - created by God and sustained in this life by His love – a love which, at its core, fosters hope. During this time of *Panic or Peace*, hope can ***still*** be evidenced in our daily lives through the adoption of at least some of the suggested behaviors shared by Louis Keene on twitter from his rabbi to the synagogue upon the arrival of the coronavirus:

One of the brand new terms that has entered our daily conversation is "social distancing". It is shorthand, as we know very well, for the practical physical precautions that we all need to and must take in order to protect ourselves and others. I'd humbly suggest though, that we use the term itself sparingly, if at all. Language is a powerful shaper of thinking. And the very last thing we need right now, is a mindset of mutual distancing. We actually need to be thinking the exact opposite way. Every hand that we don't shake must become a phone call that we place. Ever embrace that we avoid must become a verbal expression of warmth and concern. Every inch and every foot that we physically place between ourselves and another, must become a thought as to how we might be of help to one another, should the need arise. It is obvious that "distancing", if misplaced or misunderstood, will take its toll not only on our community's strength and resiliency, but upon the very integrity and meaning of our spiritual commitment.
Rav Yosef Kanefsky

My childhood pastor in Memphis, Dr. Robert G. Lee (for whom I was named), taught that "nothing lies beyond the reach of prayer except that which lies outside the will of God." Therefore, to say the least, the signs of the times called for the most honest and heartfelt prayers I could muster. To shut oneself in a prayer closet for supplication and self-examination was not difficult to accomplish, since most activities outside the home had been severely curtailed. I was surprised to find that the person with whom I was spending so much alone time (namely, myself) was not the person I thought I was, without the distractions and the busyness of life that was the absorber of my soul's activities and identity. John Bunyan's words: *I have often thought that the best Christians are found in the worst of times* did not relate to me as far as I was concerned. When I now entered my quiet times of prayer and meditation, I was driven there more often from desperation and boredom - just longing not to feel alone. Perhaps it is put best by American author and theologian, Howard Thurman, in a meditation from The Inward Journey, and posted on YouTube (Arias Williams Aug. 10, 2011) when he asks those of us in similar circumstance, "What Do You Want, Really?"

In Thy presence we become aware of many divisions within the inner circle of the self. When we enter into communion with Thee we are never sure of the voice that speaks within us. We do not always know which voice is the true voice. Sometimes it is a clear call of the heart remembering an unfulfilled hunger from other days. Sometimes it is but an echo of some failing impulse to good which we had pushed aside that a private end may triumph even in the face of the distinct call of truth. Often it is the muttering of needs that do not shape themselves in words because they are one with all the ebb and flow of every passing day. At times, the voice is like a clarion rising above all conflicts and confusions, so uttering the need for courage to stand against some evil to witness for the good, where the cost is high and the penalty great. Sometimes the voice is muted; sometimes telling us of hopes unrealized and dreams that will not rest until they incarnate themselves in us. All the while we pull back but they will not let us go. In the midst of all the sounds rising above all the mingled words, there is a strange voice but not quite a stranger...When all is still at a deeper level of silence, in soundless movement there floats up through all the chambers of being, encompassing all the tongued cries from many selves...one word: God. And the answer is the same, filling all the living silence before thy face: God . . . God.

The book title, *Cast Your Net Again...For Such a Time as This*, lays the groundwork for the soul's outcry to hear the voice of God amid all the other voices to provide connection, comfort and direction in life. I knew that I could not be alone in my fears and frustrations trying to work out my faith in the uncertainties of life during a pandemic. Whenever the answers to any questions were not forthcoming, I was reminded by the Holy Spirit to trust God and believe I would receive, so I continued to trust the *net* for His provision. Not surprisingly the net's proceeds yielded a book, the title of which is derived from the following two scriptures:

The first scripture is from the New Testament: John 21:1, 6: "After these things Jesus shewed himself *again* to the disciples at the sea of Tiberias… And he said unto them, **Cast the net** on the right side of the ship, and ye shall find." Casting on the "right" side of the ship was not the most important lesson of the day. Implicit in Jesus' instruction is that one's trust placed in the Word of God is paramount to accomplish His will in this life. The second scripture is a reply from Queen Esther to Mordecai found in Esther 4:14 of the Old Testament: "and who knoweth whether thou art come to the kingdom **for such a time as this**?" Moreover, the book's subtitle: *From Grace to Glory* outlines the journey of receiving the initial enlightening or "grace" from hearing God's voice, through the spiritual stages and wonders of living and worshipping in His Presence, until reaching the eternal reality of abiding with Him forever in the Glory of Heaven.

It is important to mention that this book is also an anthology of scriptures, quotations and reflective writings. As an artist and singer/song writer, I also felt it important to include visual and auditory tools as integral parts of this worship resource. A download link for each of the ten songs I have written, and/or arranged and sung can be found at the bottom of each page of song lyrics. Working together, the individual elements of the book are designed to enhance the provincial nature of humanity's various, yet consistent responses to the joys, sorrows and trials of life. In addition, they provide a network of faith grips to aid the journey of the follower of the Truth of God as revealed in the person of Jesus Christ, His Son. One will also find pages on which to journal regarding the invitation to experience the question contained in the soul's search for meaning: "What do I want, Really?"

Dear God,

I enter this day with joy knowing you are with me every step of the way, knowing there is a purpose to each breath that I take, knowing there is a hope toward which I walk.

I enter this day with faith knowing you are the strength which I depend on, knowing you are the love that is all embracing, know it is your peace which calms my soul.

I enter this day with praise knowing that I worship with service as with voice, hoping that my words might reveal your truth, hoping that your grace might touch another heart. Amen.

(Author Unknown)

This Little Light of Mine by Lori Pittenger

Scripture

"In the beginning was the Word, and the Word was with God, and the Word was God. The same was in the beginning with God. All things were made by him; and without him was not any thing made that was made. In him was life; and the life was the light of men...And the Word was made flesh, and dwelt among us, (and we beheld his glory, the glory as of the only begotten of the Father,) full of grace and truth." John 1:1-4, 14

"In the beginning God created the heavens and the earth and the earth was without form, and void; and darkness was upon the face of the deep. And the Spirit of God moved upon the face of the waters. And God said, Let there be light: and there was light." Genesis 1:1-3

"Deep calleth unto deep at the noise of thy waterspouts: all thy waves and thy billows are gone over me." Psalm 42:7

"And God is able to make all grace abound toward you; that ye, always having all sufficiency in all things, may abound to every good work." II Cor. 9:8

Prayer and Reflection

Holy Spirit, mighty word of God inhabit our darkness, brood over our abyss and speak to our chaos; that we may breathe with your life and share your creation in the power of Jesus Christ. Amen. Janet Morley

Jesus is the yes to every promise of God. William Barclay

The will of God will never take us where the grace of God cannot sustain us.
Billy Graham

For grace is given not because we have done good works, but in order that we may be able to do them. St. Augustine

Vortex of the Christ by Daniel Bonnell

The painting by Daniel Bonnell shown on the previous page entitled: Vortex of the Christ, might seem to be at first an odd name for a painting but when we understand the meaning of the noun-like verb vortex, that is - swirling from the center with energy and creativity coming alive from unseen depths, the image graphically portrays not only the meaning of a vortex but also the title of the painting. It is the image of the crucified Christ slain before the foundation of the world from which the vortex of life and salvation springs (Col. 1:16-20)

Related to the subtitle of this book **From Grace to Glory**, there should be no surprise that its first chapter is entitled, **Grace.** In the words of Frederick Buechner:

> The grace of God means something like: Here is your life. You might never have been, but you are because the party would not have been complete without you. Here is the world. Beautiful and terrible things will happen. Don't be afraid. I am with you. Nothing can ever separate us. It's for you I created the universe. I love you. It's only one catch. Like any other gift, the gift of grace can be yours only if you'll reach out and take it. Maybe being able to reach out and take it is a gift too…Grace is something you can never get; it but can only be given. There is no way to earn it or deserve it or bring it about any more than you can deserve the taste of raspberries and cream or earn good looks or bring about your own birth. A good sleep is grace and so are good dreams. Most tears are grace. The smell of rain is grace. Somebody loving me is grace. Loving somebody is grace. Have you ever *tried* to love somebody? A crucial eccentricity of the Christian faith is the assertion that people are saved by grace. There's nothing **you** have to do. There's nothing you **have** to do. There's nothing you have to ***do***.

It is only by God's grace – His unmerited favor - that our spirits are enlightened…Only by the power of God's great love for His creation evidenced by the sending His Son in sacrificial death for the sins of the world can the revelation of who and what we are be received and understood. In fact, it is the grace of God that enables us to even respond to His overture of love in faith and commitment to the work of Christ and The Holy Spirit in our hearts.

The reader should also not be surprised at the song choice for Chapter One of this book – ***Amazing Grace*** by John Newton. According to Henry J. M. Nouwen in ***Making All Things New***:

> *Our first task is to dispel the vague murky feeling of our discontent and to look critically at how we are living our lives. This requires honesty, courage, and trust. We must honestly unmask and courageously confront our many self-deceptive games. We must trust that our honesty and courage will lead us not to despair, but to a new heaven and a new earth.*

The lyrics of ***Amazing Grace*** describe well the condition of the soul of humanity. A short summary might be…We are blind wretches, lost in sin but through God's grace we can see and believe…saved into the light of forgiveness leading us homeward to heaven.

You are invited to enter the link at the bottom of the song lyrics page to listen and perhaps sing along with this beloved hymn written in 1772 by the Englishman, John Newton. From a lonely child and troubled young adult, he grew to become a slave ship master, bringing slaves from Africa to England. He began his conversion to Christianity experiencing God's saving grace at sea, when during a violent storm, he cried out to God to save them from certain death. Thereafter, this ship master devoted the rest of his life to God and His service, turning from slave trader to priest and notable preacher who authored some 280 hymns.

Coupled with the song lyrics to Amazing Grace there is an image of a painting entitled: *Jesus Calms the Storm.* Scripture tells us the story in Mark 4:35-41:

"And the same day, when the even was come, he saith unto them, Let us pass over unto the other side. And when they had sent away the multitude, they took him even as he was in the ship. And there were also with him other little ships. And there arose a great storm of wind, and the waves beat into the ship, so that it was now full. And he was in the hinder part of the ship, asleep on a pillow: and they awake him, and say unto him, Master, carest thou not that we perish? And he arose, and rebuked the wind, and said unto the sea, Peace, be still. And the wind ceased, and there was a great calm. And he said unto them, Why are ye so fearful? how is it that ye have no faith? And they feared exceedingly, and said one to another, What manner of man is this, that even the wind and the sea obey him?"

It is the grace of God that confronts and stills the storm to save the lives of the disciples being tossed about on turbulent seas. Likewise, before having an encounter with the saving Christ, we are helpless and tossed about by our natures bent on sinning and the consequent choices we are making in our daily lives. It is that same grace which, as with John Newton, also intervenes to calm the storm in our souls so that we can have eyes to see the truth and love of God by way of relationship with His dear Son, the Savior of the world.

In **The Spiritual Life**, Evelyn Underhill declares that: *Our spiritual life is His affair, because, whatever we may think to the contrary, it is really produced by His steady attraction and our humble and self-forgetful response to it. It consists in being drawn at His pace and in His way, to the place where He wants us to be; not the place we fancied for ourselves.* I never fancied for myself the situation brought on by a pandemic where the landscape of my life's calling as a church music director would so suddenly be eliminated and I would by God's grace then be led to author this book – **For Such a Time as This**…His Grace is indeed, Amazing…

Jesus Calms the Storm by Daniel Bonnell

Amazing Grace
Words by John Newton, Music: New Britain, Arr. Basil Alter

Amazing grace! How sweet the sound
That saved a wretch like me!
I once was lost, but now am found;
Was blind, but now I see.

'Twas grace that taught my heart to fear,
And grace my fears relieved;
How precious did that grace appear,
The hour I first believed.

Through many dangers, toils and snare,
I have already come;
'Tis grace hath brought me safe thus far,
And grace will lead me home.

When we've been there ten thousand years,
Bright shining as the sun;
We've no less days to sing God's praise
Than when we first begun.

Music Hyperlink - https://cast.jacobsladdercdc.org/home/amazing

Grace Reflections 20__

Grace Reflections 20__

Grace Reflections 20__

Grace Reflections 20__

This Little Light of Mine by Lori Pittenger

Scripture

"Thou wilt keep him in perfect peace, whose mind is stayed on thee: because he trusteth in thee." Isaiah 26:3

"And let the peace of God rule in your hearts, to the which also ye are called in one body; and be ye thankful." Colossians 3:15

"Those things, which ye have both learned, and received, and heard, and seen in me, do: and the God of peace shall be with You." Philippians 4:9

"Peace I leave with you, my peace I give unto you: not as the world giveth, give I unto you. Let not your heart be troubled, neither let it be afraid."
John 14:27

Prayer and Reflection

Think through me, thoughts of God; My Father, quiet me, Till in Thy holy presence, hushed I think Thy thoughts with Thee. Amy Carmichael

Whatever may be the tensions and the stresses of a particular day, there is always lurking close at hand the trailing beauty of forgotten joy or unremembered peace."
Howard Thurman

Speak to Him, thou for He hears, and Spirit with Spirit can meet --
Closer is He then breathing, and nearer than hands and feet.
Alfred Lord Tennyson

Peace, peace, wonderful peace, coming down from the Father above; Sweep over my spirit forever, I pray in fathomless billows of love.
Warren D. Cornell

Nothing can calm our souls more or better prepare us for life's challenges than time spent alone with God. Billy Graham

Touch by Jelena Jovanovic

...Jesus knelt to share with Thee
The silence of eternity,
Interpreted by love.
Drop Thy still dews of quietness,
Till all our strivings cease;
Take from our souls the strain and stress,
And let our ordered lives confess
The beauty of Thy peace.
John Greenleaf Whittier

The painting entitled *Touch* by Jelena Javanovic invokes the following prayer words in my soul...*Father God, we need your healing touch.* The beauty of God's peace is brush-stroked on the canvas of our lives in caring colors of concern and compassion. I am reminded of the words of Kate McIlhagga, a minister and a member of the Iona Community until her death in 2002:

God of the heights and the depths we bring to you
   those given into the desert,
   those struggling with difficult decisions.
May they choose life.

God of the light and darkness we bring to you
   those lost in the mist of drugs or drink,
   those dazzled by the use of power
May they choose life.

God of the wild beast and the ministering angel, we bring to you
   those savaged by others' greed,
   those exhausted by caring for others
May they feel your healing touch.

This chapter's title is **Peace** – what we long for but seem to come up short in our strivings…Peace - so readily identified due to our lack of it. Peace - to sleep in the thunderstorm …and not just a good night's rest or the absence of war in the world but the peace which passes understanding residing in our souls. (Philippians 4:7) It is true that "God cannot give us a happiness and peace apart from Himself, because it is not there. There is no such thing." (C.S. Lewis) The peace we require is a peace not manufactured from within ourselves because of our mindset and emotional focus, but *the* peace we receive from our Creator God. God's peace, however, does have a price – surrender in solitude. It is what we most fear...The *terrible thing, the almost impossible thing, is to hand over your whole self – all your wishes and precautions – to Christ.* (C. S. Lewis)

All of humanity seeks peace and embraces it in whatever form it presents. I was the first-born in our family and we moved to a farm outside of Memphis, Tennessee when I was only a few weeks old. There were setbacks living in the small farmhouse, as I was told when I got to be older. Lack of proper heat and only one bedroom meant there was no room for a crib, so my bed was a dresser drawer for a good while. Whether it had to do with sleeping in a dresser drawer as an infant or perhaps it was just my nature not wanting to be forcibly contained in a small space, I have always longed for the peace which comes from not feeling alone and trapped with myself. I had no siblings for a number of years, so I am sure the daily presence of my mother and the animals on the farm provided a peace to me which gave a balance to my **don't fence me in** nature.

My lone and rebellious tendencies were real however, and they did not serve me well as I grew up. I made many wrong choices, but one choice, which seemed to have *chosen me*, was my love of music so learned from my mother, who was of course, a gifted musician. I failed to mention, in my telling of the saga about the farmhouse, that my father bought a baby grand piano for my mother. Other than the animals, it was central to our lives and occupied the living space just outside the kitchen in our small farmhouse. The centrality of music in my life was not only logistical but spiritual, for music became the medium by which I experienced God's Presence and Peace. Over the years as a musician, singer and songwriter, I learned that God first beckons me to the place of solitude where in His Presence I am never alone, and it is at that time the music flows in and then through me for my good and His glory. Thanks be to God…"If chosen souls could never be alone, in deep mid-silence open-doored to God, no greatness ever had been dreamed or done." (James Russell Lowell)

"Without solitude it is virtually impossible to live a spiritual life. Solitude begins with a time and place for God, and him alone. If we really believe not only that God exists but also that he is actively present in our lives - healing, teaching, and guiding - we need to set aside a time and space to give him our undivided attention. Jesus says, *Go to your private room and, when you have shut your door, pray to your Father who is in that secret place.*" Matt. 6:6 CSV (Henry J. M. Nouwen)

When you listen to the following song, A Quiet Room, with adapted lyrics from Leslie Weatherhead set to music, please reflect on your response to God's touch in your life…Do you rise up and follow Him so that your heart's prayer agrees with F. B. Meyer…*If this day I should get lost amid the perplexities of life and the rush of many duties, do Thou search me out, gracious Lord, and bring me back into the quiet of Thy presence.*

The Right Hand of St. Francis by Daniel Bonnell

A Quiet Room
(Lyrics adapted from Leslie Weatherhead)
Music by Lana Lee Marler, Arr. Jeremey Johnson

Lord, I have made a quiet room in my heart.

Let the hush of Your Presence fall on me now.

And let the certainty of Your love

Take away my fears,

So let me rising up now,

I follow You;

So let me rising up now,

I follow You.

Music Hyperlink - https://cast.jacobsladdercdc.org/home/quiet

Peace Reflections 20__

Peace Reflections 20__

Peace Reflections 20__

Peace Reflections 20__

PROVISION

This Little Light of Mine by Lori Pittenger

Scripture

"The Lord is my shepherd; I shall not want. He maketh me to lie down in green pastures: he leadeth me beside the still waters. He restoreth my soul: he leadeth me in the paths of righteousness for his name's sake. Yea, though I walk through the valley of the shadow of death, I will fear no evil: for thou art with me; thy rod and thy staff they comfort me. Thou preparest a table before me in the presence of mine enemies: thou anointest my head with oil; my cup runneth over. Surely goodness and mercy shall follow me all the days of my life: and I will dwell in the house of the Lord for ever." Psalm 23

"Consider the lilies how they grow: they toil not, they spin not; and yet I say unto you, that Solomon in all his glory was not arrayed like one of these. If then God so clothe the grass, which is to day in the field, and tomorrow is cast into the oven; how much more will he clothe you, O ye of little faith? And seek not ye what ye shall eat, or what ye shall drink, neither be ye of doubtful mind. For all these things do the nations of the world seek after: and your Father knoweth that ye have need of these things. But rather seek ye the kingdom of God; and all these things shall be added unto you." Luke 12:27-31

Prayer and Reflection

I hand over to your care, Lord, my soul and my body, my mind and thoughts, my prayers and my hopes, my health and my work, my life and my death, my parents and my family, my friends and my neighbors, my country and all people today and forever. Amen. Lancelot Andrewes

God, of your goodness, give me yourself; for you are enough for me. I cannot properly ask anything less, to be worthy of you. If I were to ask less, I should always be in want. In you alone do I have all.

Julian of Norwich

Consider the Lilies by Lori Wright Mackert

Elie Wiesel, Holocaust survivor and author of *Night*, reminds us: "If the only prayer you say through your life is 'Thank You,' then that will be enough." Even more so than *God is great, God is good, let us thank Him for our food* (Anonymous), or *Thank you for the world so sweet; Thank you for the food we eat, Thank you for the birds that sing; Thank you, God, for everything* (E. Rutter Leatham), the Johnny Appleseed Blessing is among the favored words of Grace many may remember from their youth. Please humor my bias including it as introductory language for the simple acknowledgement of gratitude for all our sustenance from God in this Chapter entitled: Provision.

The Lord is good to me, and so I thank the Lord,
For giving me the things I need, the sun and the rain and the apple seed,
The Lord is good to me. (Anonymous)

…The Lord is good to me…I know what *good* is for this reason alone - that God is a **good** God. John Greenleaf Whittier writes: *Yet, in the maddening maze of things, And tossed by storm and flood, To one fixed trust my spirit clings; I know that God is good.* There is an Old Testament story in which Abraham is put to the test as to whether or not he believes God to be a good God. *Jehovah-Jireh*, is one of the most definitive names for God…in the Hebrew it is *Yahweh-Yireh* which means: The Lord will provide. The following account is found in Genesis 22 and documents Abraham as having ascribed that name to God:

"And he said, Take now thy son, thine only son Isaac, whom thou lovest, and get thee into the land of Moriah; and offer him there for a burnt offering upon one of the mountains which I will tell thee of. And Abraham rose up early in the morning, and saddled his ass, and took two of his young men with him, and Isaac his son, and clave the wood for the burnt offering, and rose up, and went unto the place of which God had told him. And Isaac spake unto Abraham his father and said, 'Behold the fire and the wood: but where is the lamb for a burnt offering?' And Abraham said, 'My son, God will provide himself a lamb for a burnt offering.' And they came to the place which God had told him of… and Abraham lifted up his eyes, and looked, and behold behind him a ram caught in a thicket by his horns: and Abraham went and took the ram, and offered him up for a burnt offering in the stead of his son. And Abraham called the name of that place Jehovah-Jireh: as it is said to this day.

Scholars of the Holy Scriptures note that resonant in Abraham's naming God Jehovah-Jireh, was the prophecy of John 1:29, "The next day John seeth Jesus coming unto him, and saith, Behold the Lamb of God, which taketh away the sin of the world." As if emerging from a dark dream, the Pieta Meditation by Daniel Bonnell, is a requiem to the confluence of God's love, pain, loss and triumph at Calvary. "If we think that this life is all there is to life, then there is no interpretation of our problems, our pain, not even of our privileges. But everything changes when we open up to the possibility that God's story is really our story too." (Max Lucado) God would provide Himself as a sacrifice to redeem the world from sin in the person of His Son, Jesus, who was without sin. From the foundation of creation God is the ultimate Provider for humanity…*not willing that any should perish but that all should come to repentance.* (II Peter 3:9) *For the wages of sin is death; but the gift of God is eternal life through Jesus Christ our Lord.* (Romans 6:23) We celebrate God's Provision when we observe the Lord's Supper: *For my flesh is meat indeed, and my blood is drink indeed. He that eateth my flesh, and drinketh my blood, dwelleth in me, and I and him. As the living Father has sent me, and I live by the Father: so he that eateth me, even he shall live by me… he that eateth of this bread shall live forever.* (John 6:55-58)

So it was Abraham who first named the Lord God, Jehovah-Jireh, but there are dozens upon dozens of scriptures which refer to God as Provider for anything and everything needed for life in this world – even eternal life. "All things were made by Him and without Him was not anything made that was made." (John 1:3) This is a truism that God the Creator **made all** that is and **provides all** for His creation (nature and its inhabitants) with the means to continue. And so it follows that as humans we have air to breathe, food to eat, water to drink and raiment to wear, bodies as well as shelters to inhabit, minds to think, plan and dream and hands to receive, to work, to love each other and to raise in praise to our Maker.

If then, God is the Creator of all things, another truism must be that we are the benefactors in God's creation – "God is no respecter of persons (Romans 2:11)… He sends rain on the just and the unjust." (Matthew 5:45) Like so many others, it was very difficult for me not to despair this past year 2021…I must confess that it rained on me in the pandemic – *a rain of pain* with job loss but also *a rain of provision* with the creation of this worship resource in its stead. I learned once again that God was my source, regardless of the circumstances. That being said, since everything comes from God and He is *the* major player in Creation, when something like loss of job or housing, worn shoes or bare cupboard, not to mention natural disasters, war or famine, disease and loss of life, or most recently a pandemic, how is it then, that the first word in our human response is: "I"? What am *I* going to do? How am *I* going to go on? *I* feel that this is unfair? *I* am so worried and afraid…Where is God in all our scenarios when these are our knee-jerk responses to the unpredictables of life? When I say, I am guilty of all the aforementioned, I am still using the word "I" as if I am on center stage when, in fact, I am not the *One* in charge.

It is a fallacy to think we control our lives. Jehovah-Jireh is our Provider - We shall not want because the Lord is our Shepherd (Ps. 23); He clothes the grass and the lilies of the field so He will clothe us as well (Luke 12:2-31); We lay down in peace and sleep for the Lord only makes us dwell in safety (Ps. 4:8). The words of Julian Norwich hold sway here: In *You* alone do I have all. The song theme for this chapter on Provision is entitled: *There is No I in You*. It speaks to the human circumstance of realizing we are **not** God in our lives. All that we have, we have received from a loving God…For it is in Him that we live, and move, and have our being. (Acts 17:28)

Pieta Meditation by Daniel Bonnell

There is No I in You
Words & Music by Lana Lee Marler, Arr. Jeremey Johnson

You lay me down to sleep and keep the soul of your lost sheep.
Eyes close to the silent rhythm of each breath so serenely giv'n.
There is no I in You; All that I have, I receive.
You alone are God and ever shall be.
There is no I in You.

You own the terror of the night
And the darkness our souls breathe in;
But Your love abides in the hopes
And dreams we believe in.
There is no I in You; All that I have, I receive;
You alone are God and ever shall be.
There is no I in You.

Because there is no I in You,
Death's dark dream shall not prevail;
The waking song of all is that Your love never fails.
There is no I in You; All that I have, I receive;
You alone are God and ever shall be.
There is no I in You.

I am not God, neither can I be.
There is no I in You.

Music Hyperlink - https://cast.jacobsladdercdc.org/home/there

Provision Reflections 20__

Provision Reflections 20__

Provision Reflections 20__

Provision Reflections 20__

This Little Light of Mine by Lori Pittenger

Scripture

"Trust in the Lord with all thine heart; and lean not unto thine own understanding. In all thy ways acknowledge him, and he shall direct thy paths."
Proverbs 3:5-6

"That he would grant you, according to the riches of his glory, to be strengthened with might by his Spirit in the inner man; That Christ may dwell in your hearts by faith; that ye, being rooted and grounded in love." Ephesians 3:16-17

"For whatsoever is born of God overcometh the world: and this is the victory that overcometh the world, even our faith." 1 John 5:4

"But Jesus said, Suffer little children, and forbid them not, to come unto me: for of such is the kingdom of heaven." Matthew 19:14

Prayer and Reflection

God, in you have I trusted; Upon you I cast my care. Even on you I throw my soul. Receive me as I throw myself upon you...Keep me when I sleep. Help me in whatever I do; Inspire in me whatever I think. You, Lord, by your grace. Amen.
Anselm of Canterbury

When we are no longer children, we are already dead.
Constantin Brancusi

You were God from eternity, you are God, and you will be God.
We rejoice that we can build on you and trust in you. Amen.
Karl Barth

Faith is laughter at the promise of a child called laughter.
Frederick Buechner

God has given us two hands, one to receive with and the other to give with.
Billy Graham

The Gift of Self by Maria Hunt

The topic of faith and faithfulness is best understood from God's perspective – the *Father* of faithfulness. We become persons of faith because God first loved us and reached out his hand of faithfulness to the world through the gift of His Son, Jesus, our Savior. Thomas Chisholm was born in a log cabin in Franklin, KY in 1866 and embraced Christianity at the age of 26. He was a man of modest means who became a newspaper editor and ordained Methodist minister. He authored 1200 poems, not the least of which was *Great is Thy Faithfulness*, based on Lamentations 3:22-23: "Because of the Lord's great love we are not consumed, for his compassions never fail. They are new every morning; great is your faithfulness." Although he was plagued with poor health later in life, Chisholm did not write this poem because he was enduring hardship and great stress. On the contrary, he purposed to write based on scripture as confirmed by his own words: "I must not fail to record here the unfailing faithfulness of a covenant-keeping God and that He has given me many wonderful displays of His providing care, for which I am filled with astonishing gratefulness." The lyrics testify his conscience:

> *Great is thy faithfulness, O God my Father;*
> *There is no shadow of turning with thee;*
> *Thou changest not, thy compassions, they fail not;*
> *As thou hast been, thou forever wilt be.*
>
> *Great is thy faithfulness! Great is thy faithfulness!*
> *Morning by morning new mercies I see;*
> *All I have needed thy hand hath provided;*
> *Great is thy faithfulness, Lord, unto me!*

One can see in the painting, *The Gift of Self* by Maria Hunt , there are many hands extended upward and downward and outward – The Father's hands as He gives Himself; And our hands as we reach for His grasp to receive His bounty, which in turn, we then can share with others for the good of all and for God's glory.

"For we walk by faith, not by sight." (2 Corinthians 5:7)

You've probably heard this for as long as you can remember…*Have faith like a child*…A child walks across a heavily trafficked intersection and never looks where he/she is going – Why? Because the hand of the accompanying parent is holding the hand of the child…with the foresight of an adult, the parent in love and faithfulness protects the child. All of us have stories and memories of how we ourselves have had the wondrous, innocent faith of a child – standing on the side of a swimming pool afraid to dive but trusting the parent's loving arms to receive; or that first day of school or summer camp when the car door opens and the mother says: "Go on now and have a nice time – Everything will be alright."

The scriptures proclaim in Galatians 6:7: "…whatsoever a man soweth that shall he also reap." So it holds that if a man sows to the good, in support of his faith in the promises of God, that he shall reap the benefits/proceeds/compensation for what he has sown. I remember the words of my father…Whenever he was faced with a circumstance or situation, the outcome of which could not be determined or controlled, his prayer and statement of faith was always "to play for time." He believed by the promises of God that in due time the reward for what he had sown in faith would be revealed. I never witnessed one of my father's statements of faith denied. I learned to trust in God as a child from my father's example of faith and steadfast love.

As noted earlier, it was French-Romanian artist and sculptor, Constantin Brancusi, who said: *When we are no longer children, we are already dead.* What makes this statement true? Children by nature trust, learn, and love - without these qualities the beauty of life cannot be recognized or appreciated, which in effect makes one dead to the world. Jesus said the same thing but in a different way: "unless you change and become like little children, you will never enter the kingdom of heaven." (Matt. 18:3) In effect, we grow up to God by virtue of the same dynamic which served to help us know as children that our parents are the givers of life to us, and so "by the same spiritual machinery, [we] can now rest in Him Who is the Lord and Giver of all Life." (Frank Lake, *Clinical Theology,* 1966) Likewise, Harriet Tubman, the Abolitionist, shared her simple faith: *I said to the Lord, I'm going to hold steady on to you, and I know you will see me through.*

The nature of faith by all accounts is simple…

Pray, just as you are led, without reasoning, in all simplicity.
Be a child, hanging on him that loves you. (John Wesley)

…And uncomplicated by mood or circumstances:

Faith is the art of holding on to things your reason has once accepted in spite of your changing moods.   (C. S. Lewis)

What is implicit in having faith, be it a child's faith or not, is the very *nature* of faith demonstrated in the following example from Matthew 8:5-13:

> "And when Jesus was entered into Capernaum, there came unto him a centurion, beseeching him, And saying, Lord, my servant lieth at home sick of the palsy, grievously tormented. And Jesus saith unto him, I will come and heal him. The centurion answered and said, Lord, I am not worthy that thou shouldest come under my roof: but speak the word only, and my servant shall be healed. For I am a man under authority, having soldiers under me: and I say to this man, Go, and he goeth; and to another, Come, and he cometh; and to my servant, Do this, and he doeth it. When Jesus heard it, he marveled, and said to them that followed, Verily I say unto you, I have not found

so great faith, no, not in Israel. And I say unto you, that many shall come from the east and west, and shall sit down with Abraham, and Isaac, and Jacob, in the kingdom of heaven. But the children of the kingdom shall be cast out into outer darkness: there shall be weeping and gnashing of teeth. And Jesus said unto the centurion, Go thy way; and as thou hast believed, so be it done unto thee. And his servant was healed in the selfsame hour."

And so, faith is something that is given and received and which, at its core, is simple in nature. Christ proclaimed that faith like a child is requisite to a saving relationship with the Father in heaven. We demonstrate this saving faith in our responses to challenging, negative and/or threatening situations in our lives. These are the times when our inner faith-child needs to stretch out a hand to grasp the hand of the Father whose hand of faith is already extended to us in love and providence. When the next circumstance requiring your faith-response presents itself, as it most surely will, the image of Jesus, the Boy by Daniel Bonnell and the accompanying song, *Just* should encourage your inner faith-child to just, ***Just.***

Jesus the Boy by Daniel Bonnell

Just

Words from Unknown Author and Lana Lee Marler
Music by Lana Lee Marler, Arr. Basil Alter

Just to be tender, just to be true,
Just to be glad the whole day through,
Just to be merciful. just to be mild,
Just to be trustful as a little child:

Just, Oh won't you just,
How can it be that "just" is enough?
Just, Oh won't you just,
When the needs of this world, they seem so tough.

Just to be gentle and kind and sweet,
Just to be helpful with willing feet,
Just to let love be our daily key,
That is God's will for you and me:

Just, Oh won't you just,
It is the Savior whom we must trust.
Just, Oh won't you just,
When we answer His call to be willing to "just."

Music Hyperlink - https://cast.jacobsladdercdc.org/home/just

Faith Reflections 20__

Faith Reflections 20__

Faith Reflections 20__

Faith Reflections 20__

This Little Light of Mine by Lori Pittenger

Scripture

"And she shall bring forth a son, and thou shalt call his name JESUS: for he shall save his people from their sins. Now all this was done, that it might be fulfilled which was spoken of the Lord by the prophet, saying, Behold, a virgin shall be with child, and shall bring forth a son, and they shall call his name Emmanuel, which being interpreted is, God with us."   Matthew 1:21

"For I am persuaded, that neither death, nor life, nor angels, nor principalities, nor powers, nor things present, nor things to come, Nor height, nor depth, nor any other creature, shall be able to separate us from the love of God, which is in Christ Jesus our Lord."   Romans 8:38-39

"For God so loved the world that he gave his only begotten Son, that whosoever believeth in him should not perish, but have everlasting live."
John 3:16

Prayer and Reflection

The best prayer is to rest in the goodness of God, knowing that, that goodness can reach right down to our lowest depth of need.   Julian of Norwich

Love always involves responsibility, and love always involves sacrifice. And we do not really love Christ unless we are prepared to face His task and to take up His Cross.   William Barclay

I live, yet not within myself, and thus I live in hope.
I die because I do not die.
I live, yet far beyond myself, In that I die of love.
For I live in the Lord, Who seized me for himself;
And when I offered my heart, He placed on it this sign:
"I die because I do not die."

St. Teresa of A'vila

Mary Standing before Gabriel by Daniel Bonnell

For with God nothing shall be impossible

"And in the sixth month the angel Gabriel was sent from God unto a city of Galilee, named Nazareth, to a virgin espoused to a man whose name was Joseph, of the house of David; and the virgin's name was Mary. And the angel came in unto her, and said, Hail, thou that art highly favoured, the Lord is with thee: blessed art thou among women. And when she saw him, she was troubled at his saying, and cast in her mind what manner of salutation this should be. And the angel said unto her, Fear not, Mary: for thou hast found favour with God. And, behold, thou shalt conceive in thy womb, and bring forth a son, and shalt call his name JESUS. He shall be great, and shall be called the Son of the Highest: and the Lord God shall give unto him the throne of his father David: And he shall reign over the house of Jacob for ever; and of his kingdom there shall be no end. Then said Mary unto the angel, How shall this be, seeing I know not a man? And the angel answered and said unto her, The Holy Ghost shall come upon thee, and the power of the Highest shall overshadow thee: therefore also that holy thing which shall be born of thee shall be called the Son of God. And, behold, thy cousin Elisabeth, she hath also conceived a son in her old age: and this is the sixth month with her, who was called barren. For with God nothing shall be impossible. And Mary said, Behold the handmaid of the Lord; be it unto me according to thy word. And the angel departed from her."

(Luke 1:26-38)

One can readily see in the image of *Mary Standing before Gabriel* by Daniel Bonnell that the event, although extraordinary, is depicted artfully as in ordinary life…drawn with colored crayons on a brown paper grocery bag. This image is helpful to me as I reflect on the ordinariness of my own life and how this visitation, of necessity, would appear. *For with God nothing shall be impossible…*even God in the guise of human flesh.

> Disguise is central to God's way of dealing with us human beings. Not because God is playing games with us but because the God Who is beyond our knowing makes Himself known in the disguise of what we can know. The Christian word for this is revelation, and the ultimate revelation came by incarnation…in order that we might see.
>
> Richard John Neuhaus

The remembrance and celebration each year of the birth of Jesus is one of joy and giving for our family as it is for all families of faith. But Christmas is also a time where experiences of loss can feel more poignant alongside the gifts and gaiety. It is this realization that strikes home regarding what is oft times the ordinariness, pain, and drudgery of our daily lives. A morning lament of Ruth Etchells sheds its light midst the glow of decorated trees and the angelic glow of Gabriel's visitation.

Lord of the morning, I do not want to rise and face this day. I am so weary of the endless round of tasks, of its tedium, of the lack of encouragement or appreciation, the weariness of grinding routine, the draining impact of constant petty criticism. And I feel so confined, Lord, by the lack of space for myself and my dreams. I feel a prisoner in my own life. Somewhere there must be freedom and light and gaiety and delight and stimulus and variety and encouragement, and a shared larger vision. But in my present way of life, Lord, God, I feel suffocated, trapped in a small dark room where the air is all but consumed.

Ruth Etchells included the aforementioned prayer in a book entitled: *Just As I Am,* published in 1994. One of my favorite Bible verses is Jeremiah 29:11 esv: "For I know the plans I have for you, declares the Lord, plans for welfare and not for evil, to give you a future and a hope." This verse was a favorite of mine before the year of pandemic and remains so since its onset, but I can only receive a future and a hope **just as I am,** against the backdrop of the brown paper grocery bag of my life. God the Father came down to us from heaven into the ordinariness of life because He wanted humankind to see the great end of His love through His Son, Jesus, the Savior of the world…*From Love…To Love His Own.*

The Hebrew name of Jesus is Yeshua which means "Yahweh [the Lord] is Salvation. And what does this mean? In Jesus, there is the Presence of God; In Jesus, there is the Power of God; In Jesus, there is Life in the Resurrected Christ and it is in the Name of Jesus we live our lives in and through Him and for His Glory. (Col. 3:17; 2 Thess. 1:12) Jesus was born to die…

"Shepherds gaze in wonder while angel voices sing;
This night of nights has come and brought the world the long-awaited King.
The earth is filled with gladness and yet the heavens weep;
For heaven's eyes can see He was born to die for me.

It must have broken God's heart for the future He could see;
Yet He formed His hands and feet knowing one day they'd be nailed to a tree.
So all the world could know it, a gift came from above;
For God so loved the world that He gave His only Son.
Jesus, Baby Jesus…With a tear of love in your eye;
Jesus, Baby Jesus…You knew you were born to die."

Barbara Mandrell
(*Born to Die*)

Jesus Wept by Daniel Bonnell

From Love…To Love
Words and Music by Lana Lee Marler
Arr. Basil Alter

Holy Savior, the angel brings good news to all,
Both heaven and earth;
Love's true salvation sings
Glad tidings of Your joyous birth.

Holy Savior, how can this be?
You chose to leave the heavenly bliss
To wear the robe of mortality
And bear sin's burden all for us.

Come in our hearts, blessed Virgin's Son
Redeemed by grace, the vict'ry won
Your love, O God pursues us still;
Grant that we may do Your will.

Holy Savior, God's Promise come
And make this heart of mine Your home.
From love to love Your own;
From love to love Your own.

Music Hyperlink - https://cast.jacobsladdercdc.org/home/from

Love Reflections 20__

Love Reflections 20__

Love Reflections 20__

Love Reflections 20__

MERCY

This Little Light of Mine by Lori Pittenger

Scripture

"For God commendeth his love toward us, in that, while we were yet sinners, Christ died for us."   Romans 5:8

"For thou, Lord, art good, and ready to forgive; and plenteous in mercy unto all them that call upon thee..."   Psalm 86:5

"Let the wicked forsake his way, and the unrighteous man his thoughts: and let him return unto the Lord, and he will have mercy upon him; and to our God, for he will abundantly pardon."   Isaiah 55:7

"For great is thy mercy toward me; and thou hast delivered my soul from the lowest hell."   Psalm 86:13

Prayer and Reflection

And all the wickedness in this world that men might work or think is no more to the mercy of God than a live coal in the sea.
               William Langland

Oh, how I love Jesus; Oh, how I love Jesus; Oh, how I love Jesus, because He 'wept' for me.
               Andrew L. Smith

You have not lived today until you have done something for someone who can never repay you.
               John Bunyan

To be convinced in our hearts that we have forgiveness of sins and peace with God by grace alone is the hardest thing.
               Martin Luther

The Father's Forgiveness by Daniel Bonnell

> Though waves and storms go o'er my head,
> Though strength, and health, and friends be gone,
> Though joys be withered all and dead, Though every comfort be withdrawn,
> On this my steadfast soul relies - Father, Thy mercy never dies! (J.A. Rothe)

The very nature of God is Love according to scripture. (I John 4:8) And as such, God's great Love reservoir houses great Mercy. God's Mercy is eternal…It never dies. Mercy flows forth from the Holiness of His abundant nature in no less fashion than the birth of all creation. God's Holiness never dies and "without holiness, no man shall see the Lord." (Hebrews 12:14) Therefore, God's Love nature requires His Mercy in the forgiveness of sins against His Holiness through the triumphant death of His Son, Jesus, over the judgment we deserved as sinners. "Only through the cross can God be just and the justifier of sinners… Jesus' blood appeases every storm, heals every wound, blots out every sin, removes every curse and makes a heavy chain into a gentle yoke." (Dr. Robert G. Lee)

I first experienced the *gentle yoke* of God's love and mercy in Sunday School when, as a child I learned the song "Jesus Loves Me" followed by "O How I Love Jesus…Because He first loved me." These are simple but profound lyrics which made their home in the recesses of hearts whose lenses were darkened by sin. By giving His Son, God came down from His glory to provide redemption for our sins - because *He first loved us.* Andrew L. Smith writes an astute variation on the beloved childhood song: "O how I love Jesus, because He 'wept' for me." *The Father's Forgiveness* portrayed by Daniel Bonnell captures that gripping moment of God's Love and Mercy experienced by the sinner saved by grace. "But God, Who is rich in mercy, for His great love wherewith He loved us, Even when we were dead in sins, hath quickened us together with Christ, (by grace ye are saved.). Ephesians 2:4-5.

As a sinner, saved by grace, the prayer of F. B. Meyer holds particular significance to me: "If my soul has turned perversely to the dark; If I have left some brother

wounded by the way; If I have preferred my aims to Thine; If I have been impatient and would not wait; If I have marred the pattern drawn out for my life; If I have cost tears to those I loved; If my heart has murmured against Thy will, O Lord, forgive."

I learned unconditional love and forgiveness from my earthly father in the quietude and daily demeanor of his interactions with others. He had such a quick mind and never waivered in his attitude of straight forward gaze and concern when approached with the needs of others. Whether it was overseas missions, a stranger in need or the timid confessions from his own children, my father was a consistent instrument of the Kingdom of God on this earth. One could never misunderstand his intent or escape the focus of his heart through his eyes in administering correction or understanding and compassion – catching a glimpse from his eyes was always enough to quicken my heart and get my attention.

Yes, God's mercy never dies! As believers in Christ, we receive God's forgiveness in our daily prayers of confession. It was just this past year, when I had a fresh reminder of the love and mercy of God through His protection when my purse was stolen in the parking lot of a shopping center. I had been standing in line to check-out for a long line and was singing to myself the lyrics to the new melody I had written for the hymn, *Turn Your Eyes Upon Jesus* which I entitled: *His Face*. When I realized that my purse had been taken just after loading my groceries in the car, I felt the glimpse of the Lord on me in that parking lot. I could not help but be quickened by those lyrics to **turn your eyes upon Jesus** in faith and gratitude for God's mercy that I had not been accosted or harmed, but was only temporarily apprehensive and inconvenienced. An important part of this experience for me was to extend true forgiveness from my heart to the person or persons who had sinned against me. The concerns of my situation *dimmed in the light of His glory and grace*. It is my prayer that the reader can *Glimpse the Christ* in this musical setting and be comforted that the challenges in life can become opportunities to experience God's mercy and in turn, extend that mercy to others.

Glimpse of the Christ by Daniel Bonnell

His Face
Words by Helen H. Lemmel and Lana Lee Marler
Music by Lana Lee Marler, Arr. Basil Alter

O my soul I am so weary and troubled; There's no light in the darkness I see.
But there is light for a look at the Savior, And life more - abundant and free.

Turn your eyes upon Jesus. Look full in His wonderful face;
And the things of this world will grow strangely dim...
In the Light of His glory and grace.

His Word shall not fail me, He promised; Believe Him, and all shall be well.
Then I'll go to a world that is dying, His perfect salvation to tell.

Turn your eyes upon Jesus. Look full in His wonderful face;
And the things of this world will grow strangely dim...
In the Light of His glory and grace.

I feel so very thankful; It makes my heart sing.
New life I have been given by the Maker of all things.
I find it hard to fathom; It's wonderful to know;
My sins are all forgiven as I look on Jesus' face;

His face…Face...His face.

Music Hyperlink - https://cast.jacobsladdercdc.org/home/his

Mercy Reflections 20__

Mercy Reflections 20__

Mercy Reflections 20__

Mercy Reflections 20__

This Little Light of Mine by Lori Pittenger

Scripture

"And being found in fashion as a man, he humbled himself, and became obedient unto death, even the death of the cross." Philippians 2:8

" Father, if thou be willing, remove this cup from me: nevertheless not my will, but thine, be done." Luke 22:42

"Not every one that saith unto me, Lord, Lord, shall enter into the kingdom of heaven; but he that doeth the will of my Father which is in heaven."
Matthew 7:21

"Then said Jesus unto his disciples, If any man will come after me, let him deny himself, and take up his cross, and follow me." Matthew 16:24

Prayer and Reflection

The things, good Lord that I pray for; give me grace to labor for.
Sir Thomas More

The greatest thing is a life of obedience in the routine things of everyday life. No amount of fine feeling can take the place of faithful doing.
William Barclay

The words of the Lord are the seed sown by the sower. Into our hearts they must fall that they may grow. Meditation and prayer must water them, and obedience keep them in the sunlight. Thus will they bear fruit for the Lord's gathering.
George MacDonald

Life's most persistent and urgent question is, 'What are you doing for others?'
Dr. Martin Luther King, Jr.

Trinity and the Cross by Daniel Bonnell

Almighty God, Whom the eye cannot behold, and Whom we cannot hear with the hearing of the ear, still let us this day feel Thy Presence and know Thy Love, and being stirred and moved above ourselves, thus be lifted into the knowledge of God and the bearing of His holy way...
George Dawson

Not only *for such a time as this* during a pandemic, but at any and all times, persons of faith would agree that to follow the example of Christ in obedience to God is critical. Dr. Martin Luther King, Jr. argued that **"the time is <u>always</u> right to do what is right."** The *Trinity and the Cross* by Daniel Bonnell is a thought-provoking image - a stark reminder and remembrance that the distinct persons of the Trinity, the Father, the Son and the Holy Spirit, were not separated at the cross of Christ. The Eternal Love at work in the Holy Trinity beckons us to follow in obedience and solidarity. Stefan Andre Waligur expresses so vividly albeit a mural in words, regarding God, the Son: "Jesus haunts me like no other. The life, death, and resurrection of Jesus blows me away. I choose to follow the Jesus who walks right through the walls of institutional religion, who turns over tables, and kicks down the gates of hell. I follow the Jesus who washed feet , who ate with outcasts, and died among criminals of the state. This is the Jesus who sings and dances with Krishna, Shakti, Buddha, Muhammad, the Goddess...all the while remaining Jesus. I guess I'm in love!" ***Love always involves responsibility, and love always involves sacrifice. And we do not really love Christ unless we are prepared to face His task and to take up His cross.*** (William Barclay)

When you look into the mirror of yourself in the cross of Christ, does your reflection likewise invoke a consonant prayer of confession and entreaty?
O loving Father, make me like Jesus:
The Jesus who could spend nights in prayer;
(Do I? ever?) half a night? three hours? one?)
The Jesus who went about doing good;
    (Is this my chief longing? or a hazy general intention?)

The Jesus who made time to talk to Nicodemus;
> (How patiently do I give time to the Nicodemus who wants to talk?
> The old lady in the shopping centre? The junior in the office?
> The elderly relative in the nursing home? The teenage children?
> My spouse? My friend?)

The Jesus who could not bear to see the mother cry at Nain:
> (Do I open myself to other people's grief, Lord?
> Or refuse the load on my heart?)

The Jesus who would not let the marriage at Cana be spoilt by lack of wine;
> (How much, Lord, am I willing to give myself to the ordinary occasions of other people's life? in time? in energy? in money? in caring?)

The Jesus who was strong enough not to answer back when accused unjustly;
> (How instinctively defensive am I, Lord, and what do I do about it?)

The Jesus who could shrink from the cup of suffering, yet drain it to the last dregs;
> (O Lord, certainly I shrink from suffering; keep me more faithful when required to endure it.)

The Jesus who could pray for the men who nailed him to the cross;
> (O Lord, I do not know how to pray for those who hurt me:
> but I do know I long to be able to. Teach me, Lord.)

O loving Father, make me like the Jesus
Who came to the world, to show what you were like. Amen.

> Based on a personal prayer of Bishop Jacob Travancore, South India

I cannot think about salvation afforded by the death of Christ for humanity without reflecting on the *Jail Cell Salvation Story* of my father-in-law, whose entire life had been one of hardship and subsequent selfishness and rebellion. The son of a dirt farmer, he left home at the age of fifteen and worked on a Mississippi Riverboat. He learned the rough and rowdiness of life while working on the boat that summer and every summer until high school graduation, whereupon he enlisted in the Navy and served his country in World War II. He learned skills in the service which enabled him to become a successful businessman, but he sorely lacked experience in family relations. Having virtually raised himself, my father-in-law, for the most part, answered to his own desires. Sadly, he and the lives of his wife and children bore the consequences of his unenlightened choices, suffering the curse of violent domestic upheaval, divorce and suicide. His health was broken from heart attack and stroke followed by hip replacement surgery, so he lived only at the behest of multiple prescriptions.

It was in the Summer of 2003, when in his mid-seventies, my father-in-law found himself falsely accused of domestic violence, was arrested on charges of resisting arrest and then taken to the local precinct where he was jailed. To say the least, this was a stressful and unfamiliar situation as he had never been previously arrested. He was alone, abandoned and without any of his prescription medicines. He suffered severely from the sudden and complete withdrawal of his meds. The chaplain called my husband from the jail out of concern. After five days in this state - having been deprived of all medicine and with no sleep, his father's condition was dire at best. In fact, all those present - guards and inmates alike - were making bets as to whether he would live until morning.

But, in the middle of the night a song began to fill the air…And the song rose from the depths of the jail cell and from the depths of my father-in-law's heart as he sang a song that no one would have guessed he even knew or could remember from his youth. It was his testimony of faith placed in the One Who died to save him from his sins: *Jesus Loves Me, This I Know.* Saint Teresa of A'vila adds her voice of solidarity: "The closer one approaches to God, the simpler one becomes." After one month's confinement, he was released from jail. He was baptized in the river near to his residence and joined a small local Baptist church. From that day forward, he lived as best he could in obedience to the Word of God and finally saw the *Unclouded Day*, when at the age of 91, he went to meet the Savior of his soul in heaven.

The lyrics of a hymn favorite written by Jessie B. Pounds in 1906 entitled: *The Way of the Cross Leads Home* testify to this salvation story. In the Gospel of John Jesus said: "I am the Way, the Truth and the Life; no one comes to the Father except through me." *Heart and Hook* by Thomas Cheatham is the name of the image adjacent to the song, *Jesus Said,* which was written by me for this Chapter entitled: Obedience. It depicts the truth that there is a *hook in the heart of love afforded by the cross of Christ* – That hook is found in His command when Jesus said: "As I have loved you, love one another." (John 13:34) His command is ever-present in all our days, and in all our ways, that we should love one another. As Christ so demonstrated to us - **to love is not just an emotion, it is an action**. In the words of C. S. Lewis: "Do not waste time bothering whether you 'love' your neighbor; act as if you do, and you will presently come to love him." The *tell* of discipleship is love. (John 13:35) "By this shall men know that you are my disciples if you have love one for another," *Jesus Said*…

Heart and Hook by Thomas Cheatham

Jesus Said
Words from New Testament Gospels Matthew and John
Music by Lana Lee Marler, Arr. Robert Totten

Jesus said: "I am the Way, the Truth and the life;
No one comes to the Father, except through Me.
I am the Good Shepherd, My sheep hear My voice,
I know My own and My own follow me."

"The first and greatest commandment is
Love the Lord your God with all your heart,
Soul, mind and strength.
The second greatest commandment is like the first,
To love your neighbor as yourself."

"As I have loved you, love one another.
This new commandment is to love one another.
By this shall men know You are My disciples,
If you have love one for another."

"By this shall men know You are My disciples,
If you have love one for another.
One for another."

Music Hyperlink - https://cast.jacobsladdercdc.org/home/jesus

Obedience Reflections 20__

Obedience Reflections 20__

Obedience Reflections 20__

Obedience Reflections 20__

HOPE

This Little Light of Mine by Lori Pittenger

Scripture

"Now the Lord is the Spirit, and where the Spirit of the Lord is, there is freedom."
2 Corinthians 3:17 ESV

"By whom also we have access by faith into this grace wherein we stand, and rejoice in hope of the glory of God. And not only so, but we glory in tribulations also; knowing that tribulation worketh patience; And patience, experience; and experience, hope."
Romans 5:2-4

"But they that wait upon the Lord shall renew their strength: they shall mount up with wings as eagles; they shall run and not be weary; they shall walk and not faint."
Isaiah 40:3

Prayer and Reflection

O my God, I have no idea where I am going. Nor do I really know myself, and the fact that I think I am following your will does not mean that I am actually doing so. But I desire to do your will, and I know the very desire pleases you. Therefore I will trust you always though I may seem to be lost. I will not fear, for you are always with me, O my dear God.
Thomas Merton

Hope opens new horizons, making us capable of dreaming what is not even imaginable.
Pope Francis

Surrender to God is a formidable adventure....He who can risk himself wholly to it finds himself directly in the hands of God, and is therefore confronted with a situation which makes "simple faith" a vital necessity; in other words, the situation becomes so full of risk or overly dangerous that the deepest instincts are aroused. An experience of this kind is always numinous, for it unites all aspects of totality.
Carl Gustav Jung

Spirit of Hope by Maria Hunt

"...where the Spirit of the Lord is, there is freedom" (2 Cor. 3:17 ESV)
Freedom to do what?...Freedom from what?

The spirit of fear hangs its dark brooding mystique over all our lives. It halts us in our tracks and impedes our strivings to learn and grow. In glowing contrast, the painting, *Spirit of Hope* by Maria Hunt, illustrates the emergence of the light and hope of the Holy Spirit into the seeming chaos of our lives. With freedom *from* fear, we are free to live, love, learn, laugh, sing, dance, dream and **hope** for the future. Most would say that they long for freedom from the fear of death. But where the Spirit of the Lord is, there is freedom...even freedom from the fear of death. "He who didn't spare his own Son, but delivered him up for us all, how would he not also with him *freely* give us all things." (Romans 8:32)

> *For Christians, hope is ultimately hope in Christ. The hope that He really is what for centuries we have been claiming He is. The hope that despite the fact that sin and death still rule the world, He somehow conquered them.* (Frederick Buechner)

When we no longer live in fear, we are then free to truly live...live our lives in belief and hope through the presence of the Spirit of God. "Now the God of **hope** fill you with all joy and peace in believing, so that ye should abound in **hope** by the power of the Holy **Spirit**." (Romans 5:13) Hope is the mason jar of fireflies we carry with us in every situation in life...And please don't laugh - I find this a helpful metaphor - to remember the thrilling glow in the darkness, a promise of light and hope for direction home. *A real spiritual life...makes us so alert and aware of the world around us, that all that is and happens becomes part of our contemplation and meditation and invites us to a free and fearless response.* (Henry J.M. Nouwen)

Whether said by Dr. Martin Luther King, Jr. in his "I Have a Dream" speech or Elie Wiesel in his book, <u>Night</u>, when he offered a prayerful release to his father who died in a concentration camp at Buchenwald, the exclamation, Free at Last! is the voice of hope which echoes triumph in the conflicts of life as well as final victory at the grave! I am reminded of the words from the refrain of *His Eye Is on the Sparrow* by Civilla D. Martin – "I sing because I'm happy; I sing because I'm free. His eye is on the sparrow and I know He watches me." My life might be best described as one of risk. I had always longed for freedom to live life on my own terms and do whatever I wanted but without the negative consequences, of course. Perhaps it was to escape the bonds of a conservative and protective environment in which I was raised, but even before I realized the formidable adventure I would be embracing by surrendering myself to God, my nature was such that the *path unknown* had a special summons for me. All that being said, one might not be wrong to project that the unusual landscape and challenges afforded to me by the sequestering required in a pandemic would serve to feed my hunger for the unusual experience. I would like to say that I welcomed the opportunity but that would not be true. I struggled to find hope in a world seemingly out of kilter and fraught with danger and death…"O Holy Spirit, descend plentifully into my heart. Enlighten the dark corners of this neglected dwelling and scatter there Thy cheerful beams."

(St. Augustine)

I will lift up mine eyes unto the hills, from whence cometh my help.
*My help cometh from the L*ORD*, which made heaven and earth.*
He will not suffer thy foot to be moved:
He that keepeth thee will not slumber.
Behold, he that keepeth Israel shall neither slumber nor sleep.
*The L*ORD *is thy keeper: the L*ORD *is thy shade upon thy right hand.*
The sun shall not smite thee by day, nor the moon by night.
*The L*ORD *shall preserve thee from all evil: he shall preserve thy soul.*
*The L*ORD *shall preserve thy going out and thy coming in*
From this time forth, and even for evermore.

Psalm 121

Out of the mountain of despair, a stone of hope (Dr. Martin Luther King, Jr.) presented itself, when I was privileged to read a poem by Carman Bernos de Gasztold entitled: *Prayer of the Goat* from "Prayers From the Ark," (1947) translated by Rumer Godden. The lyrics of this poem most dramatically described who I had always been and continued to be in my relationship with the Lord of Glory. Wild goats are sure-footed and nimble creatures, leaping from rock to rock to dangerous heights without falling – equipped by God to thrive in the heights where others wouldn't venture, but for which they were fashioned. I readily identified with the validity of this poem as it related to my life. As I read the words of the poem, it seemed that the melody already existed by which to incorporate them into song – I heard the music in my head and began singing it as I read…the rest is history. When I shared this newfound insight with my siblings, they were repelled that I would look at myself as a goat…"you are a sheep" they decried. I had to disagree with them, big surprise, and perhaps you will find yourself in agreement with me when you read and listen to the *Prayer of the Goat* - **Lord, let me live as I will; I need a little wild freedom. Lord, let me live as an adventurer, quivering with delight on the summit of the world**. *Hope in the Heights* is the title of the accompanying painting by Daniel Bonnell. Perhaps you may discover for yourself, in this image and song, that Christ is your Hope in the Heights!

> ***A person of hope can hear music in the suffering.***
> (Andrew L. Smith)

Hope in the Heights by Daniel Bonnell

Prayer of the Goat
Adapted by Lana Lee Marler from poem by Carman Bernos de Gasztold
Music: Ebenezer Tune by Thomas John Williams, Arr. Basil Alter

Lord, let me live as I will. I need a little wild freedom.
A little giddiness of heart; The strange taste of unknown flowers.

For whom are Your lofty mountains?
Your snow wind? These springs?
Lord, let me live as I will,
To delight on the summit of the world.

Lord, let me live as I will.
I love to bound to the heart of
All Your marvels, leap your chasms;
My mouth stuffed with intoxicating grass.

Lord, the sheep do not understand.
They graze and graze all in the same direction.

Lord, let me live as an adventurer,
Quivering with delight
On the summit of the world.

Music Hyperlink - https://cast.jacobsladdercdc.org/home/prayer

Hope Reflections 20__

Hope Reflections 20__

Hope Reflections 20__

Hope Reflections 20__

This Little Light of Mine by Lori Pittenger

Scripture

"Likewise, I say unto you, there is joy in the presence of the angels of God over one sinner that repenteth."   Luke 15:10

"Whom having not seen, ye love; in whom, though now ye see him not, yet believing, ye rejoice with joy unspeakable and full of glory: Receiving the end of your faith, even the salvation of your souls."   1 Peter 1:8-9

"Thou wilt shew me the path of life: in thy presence is fulness of joy; at thy right hand there are pleasures for evermore."   Psalm 16:11

Prayer and Reflection

Lord, you came to give us life, and life that was more abundant. Help me not to turn away from life but to follow your spirit, to accept the thorn as well as the flower, and to be grateful for the gift of life.
    Frank Topping

During my childhood – I slept in bed. During the adolescence – I waited at the door. In my maturity – I have flown toward the heavens!
    Constantin Brancusi

Lord...May your bounty teach me greatness of heart. May your magnificence stop me being mean. Seeing you a prodigal and open-handed giver, let me give unstintingly like a King's son like God's own.   Archbp Helder Camara

So heaven is torn open above us humans, and the joyful message of God's salvation in Jesus Christ rings out from heaven to earth as a cry of joy. I believe, and in believing I receive Christ; I have everything. I live before God.
    Dietrich Bonhoeffer

The Prodigal and the Father by Daniel Bonnell

Joy is the simplest form of gratitude.
(Karl Barth)

The story of the prodigal son found in Luke 15:11-32 recounts the familiar story of the journey of a willful son who left home and made many wrongful choices. In despair, the son realized the error of his ways when he was facing death as a consequence of the direction his choice of journey had taken him. In humility the son repented and then made the *right* choice to journey homeward to his father, whereupon with open embrace in **joy** and gladness, the father forgave his son and welcomed him back home. Please note the sorrowful stance of the son in Daniel Bonnell's *The Prodigal and the Father* and the warm, compassionate embrace of the father. The lost son, the prodigal, repented and returned home and, in so doing, learned the true meaning of love and joy.

> I got lost along the way; The path was full of briars and stones. I walk slowly now and my feet are bloody. But I have discovered the miracle of life is that even with bloody feet I can still love...In fact bloody feet do not hurt now nearly as much as they used to. (Andrew L. Smith)

We are all on a journey...either toward the light of God or away from it. What the journey is and where it ends depends on the choices we make. According to Isaiah 53:6, All of us are lost...*All we like sheep have gone astray; we have turned every one to his own way; and the LORD hath laid on him the iniquity of us all.* When we journey with Jesus, having placed our life and will by faith in the saving grace of His shed blood for our sins, then we journey toward our eternal home with Him...*Looking unto Jesus the author and finisher of our faith; who for the **joy** that was set before him endured the cross, despising the shame, and is set down at the right hand of the throne of God.* (Hebrews 12:2)

In the parable of the prodigal son, the father represents God the Father who, for the *joy* that was set before him," endured the pain of separation from His Son because of sin. The *joy* of the assurance that His son would return in hope and love, prompted the father to give his son freedom of choice to leave on his willful journey in the first place.

There is a well-known saying that, it is the journey that counts, not necessarily the destination. But with God, both are important. However, God does not guarantee that the journey will be without occasions for bumps, bruises and missteps…God does however, promise to be with us every step we take and comfort and guide us on our way. We are taught in Nehemiah 8:10 that "the joy of the Lord is your strength." This "joy" is more than an emotion – not just a feeling of happiness. It is not a joy perceived from clicking our heels together and confidently declaring, "There's no place like home!" **The "Joy" of the Lord is the *state of being with the Lord*** in complete confidence on the journey and assurance for the destination.

> We place ourselves and all that we lack and that the world requires in your hands. Our hope is in you. We trust in you. You have never let your people be put to shame, whenever they earnestly called on you. What you have begun, you will surely finish. Amen.
>
> (Karl Barth)

Scripture is in agreement with Karl Barth's prayer. In Philippians 1:6 we read: "Being confident of this very thing, that he which hath begun a good work in you will perform it until the day of Jesus Christ." But let us also be reminded that as followers of Christ and sojourners with Him, we have responsibilities on the journey - a requisite admonition to "work out our own salvation with fear and trembling."(Phil. 2:12) George Beverly Shea offered a song written by Ruth Caye Jones (published 1944) at many of the Billy Graham Crusades. Appropriately entitled: *In Times Like These,* it is a poignant reminder to heed this admonition on our journey – not only *for such a time as this,* but for all times.

The song lyrics are simple and declarative:
In times like these, you need a Savior;
> In times like these, you need an anchor.
Be very sure, be very sure, your anchor holds and grips the solid rock.
> This Rock is Jesus, Yes, He's the One; This Rock is Jesus, The only One.

Just before the end of WW II in 1945, thirty-nine year old Dietrich Bonhoeffer, German Lutheran Pastor, Theologian and modern Christian martyr to the faith, testified to his journey shortly before being hung as a war criminal in a concentration camp:

> How should one become arrogant over successes or shaken by one's failures when one shares in God's suffering in the life of this world?...I am grateful that I have been allowed this insight, and I know that it is only on the path that I have finally taken that I was able to learn this. So I am thinking gratefully and with peace of mind about past as well as present things...May God lead us kindly through these times, but above all, may God lead us to himself.

"May God lead us kindly through these times, but above all, may God lead us to himself" – a testament to enduring extreme hardship on the journey, but all the while experiencing joyful confidence in the grace, love, hope, provision and presence of God. In 1738, some two hundred years earlier, the great hymn writer, Charles Wesley, wrote the words in similar testament to the amazing love and providence of God on our faith journey for his hymn entitled: *And Can It Be That I Should Gain*. His words have been adapted to a musical arrangement of my own for this Chapter on *Joy*. It is my prayer, as well, for the reader to find that ***the joy of the Lord is your strength*** for the journey on **The Road Home**…

The Road Home by Daniel Bonnell

Amazing Love…How Can It Be?
Adapted Lyrics from Charles Wesley and Music by Lana Lee Marler
Arr. Basil Alter

Jesus left His Father's throne above,
So free, so infinite His grace;
Emptied Himself of all but love,
And bled for Adam's helpless race.

Amazing love! How can it be
That Thou, my God should die for me?
Died He for me, who caused His pain.
For me, who Him to death pursued.

Long my imprisoned spirit lay
Fast bound in sin and nature's night;
Thine eye diffused a quick'ning ray,
I woke, the dungeon flamed with light.

My chains fell off, my heart was free;
I rose, went forth and followed Thee.
No condemnation now I dread;
Jesus, and all in Him is mine!

Alive in Him, my living Head
And clothed in righteousness divine.
Bold I approach th'eternal throne,
And claim the crown, through Christ my own.

Music Hyperlink - https://cast.jacobsladdercdc.org/home/love

Joy Reflections 20__

Joy Reflections 20__

Joy Reflections 20__

Joy Reflections 20__

GLORY

This Little Light of Mine by Lori Pittenger

Scripture

"And I saw a new heaven and a new earth: for the first heaven and the first earth were passed away; and there was no more sea. And I, John, saw the holy city, new Jerusalem, coming down from God out of heaven, prepared as a bride adorned for her husband. And I heard a great voice out of heaven saying, Behold, the tabernacle of God is with men, and he will dwell with them, and they shall be his people, and God himself shall be with them, and be their God. And God shall wipe away all tears from their eyes; and there shall be no more death, neither sorrow, nor crying, neither shall there be any more pain: for the former things are passed away. And he that sat upon the throne said, Behold, I make all things new."

Revelation 21:1-5

Prayer and Reflection

Bring me, O Lord God, at my last awakening, into the house and gate of heaven, to enter into that gate and dwell in that house, where there shall be no darkness nor dazzling but one equal light; no noise nor silence but one equal music; no fears nor hopes but one equal possession; no ends nor beginnings but one equal eternity; in the habitations of thy glory and dominion world without end. Amen.

John Donne

Christ is the morning star Who when the darkness of this world is past
Brings to his saints the promise of the Light of life and opens everlasting day.

The Venerable Bede

I am not going to die, I'm going home like a shooting star.

Sojourner Truth

For the Christian, heaven is where Jesus is. We do not need to speculate on what heaven will be like. It is enough to know that we will be forever with Him.

William Barclay

Night is drawing nigh: For everything that has been, thanks.
To everything that will be, yes.

Dag Hammarskjold
U.N. General Secretary

Vortex of the Christ by Daniel Bonnell

"…Eye hath not seen, nor ear heard, neither have entered into the heart of man, the things which God hath prepared for them that love him." I Corinthians 2:9

Great, Holy, and merciful God, we yearn for your ultimate revelation, in which it will be clear to all that the whole created world and all of history, all people and their life stories were, are, and will be in your gracious and strict hand.
(Karl Barth)

All that is, and ever shall be, was birthed through the Grace of our Creator God. I invite you to gaze upon the pictorial representation of the crucified Christ slain before the foundation of the world from which the vortex of life and salvation springs. "Deep calleth unto deep at the noise of thy waterspouts: all thy waves and thy billows are gone over me." (Ps. 42:7) All of creation thirsts for the Presence of God *as a deer pants for flowing streams of water, so pants my soul for you, O God*. (Ps. 42:1 NIV) In concert with all of creation, David the Psalmist calls out from his place of profound need for the unsurpassed power of God…***deep calls unto deep***. The depth of the power and love of God has no limits… likewise, the depth of need which His power and love can remedy has no boundaries.

Martin Luther described *Vortex of the Christ* by Daniel Bonnell without ever seeing it…

This grace of God is a very great, strong, mighty and active thing.
It does not lie asleep in the soul. Grace hears, leads, drives, draws, changes,
Works all in man, and lets itself be distinctly felt and experienced.
It is hidden, but its works are evident.

The works of the Grace of God are profoundly evident and they will not remain hidden…
For the Lord himself shall descend from heaven with a shout, with the voice of the archangel, and with the trump of God: and the dead in Christ shall rise first:
Then we which are alive and remain shall be caught up together with them in the clouds, to meet the Lord in the air: and so shall we ever be with the Lord.
(I Thessalonians 4:16-17)

By God's Grace you have journeyed from *Grace to Glory* in this worship resource.

Enter this door

As if the floor

Within were gold,

And every wall

Of jewels all

Of wealth untold;

As if a choir

In robes of fire

Were singing here.

Nor shout, nor rush,

But hush…

For God is here.

(The Rev. James MacKay)

…But hush…God is here…
In the stillness, the words of American author and theologian, Howard Thurman, in a meditation from *The Inward Journey* resonate anew:

What do you want, really?

Thurman's conclusion was that the voices in our heads answer in similitude…**God.**

A popular hymn written in 1907 by Ada R. Habershon offers congregations occasion to voice answers to the heart's question: **What Do You Want, Really?**

> Will the circle be unbroken
> By and by, Lord, by and by
> There's a better home-a-waiting
> In the sky, Lord, in the sky.

There is an ancient concept of prayer, whether in praise or petition, which is meant to help foster the awareness of the Presence of God. In The Breath of Life: A Simple Way to Pray, Ron DelBene explains that this individualized short breath prayer is "a way to have on our lips what is always in our heart." A breath prayer has the unique character of the unbroken circle. While breathing in, one recites their preferred name for God and then, breathing out, the prayer of praise or petition is offered. I discovered my own simple breath prayer which has ever echoed from my heart as follows:

Lord Jesus, please hold me close to You.

It would seem that Edwin Hatch's breath prayer found an extension in the hymn lyrics his heart crafted for *Breathe on Me, Breath of God*:

Breathe on me, Breath of God;
Fill me with life anew,
That I may love what Thou dost love,
And do what Thou wouldst do.

Breathe on me, Breath of God,
Till I am wholly Thine,
Until this earthly part of me
Glows with Thy fire divine.

Breathe on me, Breath of God,
Until my heart is pure,
Until with Thee I will one will,
To do and to endure.

Breathe on me, Breath of God;
So shall I never die,
But live with Thee the perfect life
Of Thine eternity.

As a singer, I am acutely aware of the significance of "breath" as a means for musical expression of *Grace and Glory* in the Kingdom of God. I did not intend to birth a song at all when I wrote the words for *O Holy Vision, Most Glorious*…I knew I was but the instrument in this work for the Kingdom…God was the author. Saint Teresa of A'vila was a Spanish Carmelite nun who lived in the 1500s. As a mystic and author, her spiritual writings include: "Christ has no body now, but yours. Yours are the eyes through which Christ looks out His compassion into the world. Yours are the feet with which Christ walks to do good. Yours are the hands with which Christ blesses the world." By God's grace let us remember that as Christ's own; "Yours are the hands with which Christ blesses the world." *Be* blessed and *be* a blessing…

> ***The wires are holding hands around the holes: To avoid breaking the ring, they hold tight the neighboring wrist, and it's thus with holes they make a fence. Lord, there are lots of holes in my life. There are some in the lives of my neighbors. But if you wish, we shall hold hands. We shall hold very tight and together we should make a fine roll of fence to adorn Paradise.*** (Michael Quoist)

In all humbleness of spirit, I would now like to share my own experience of religious ecstasy which birthed the lyrics and then the song for the final Chapter entitled: Glory…

My husband and I had succumbed to the temptation of becoming middle-aged hippies. We purchased a small van, placed a double-size mattress in the back, and began to make expeditions out west whenever we had two weeks' vacation time. The vision was mine alone, as we made our way between Fort Benton and Great Falls, Montana. It was nearing dusk when we crested a hill and God gave me a vision of the outskirts of heaven…No words can I recall to describe the experience I saw would be adequate. Suffice it to say that I felt transported into that reality – a reality that my husband did not see sitting beside me in the driver's seat of the van.

I was so awe-struck and moved, that God came to me in a vision the next night while I slept, and sat beside me at the foot of my bed, in order to comfort me and reinforce my experience granted in His providence.

It would be two years later in the Fall of 2020, when we were on a similar journey out west, that God impressed upon me the need to document in words the import of my experience of the outskirts of heaven. For a couple of days, we traveled in virtual silence and the heavenly script surfaced from God's spirit to my own spirit. The lyrics reflect from my inner core the revelation of hope and glory…what I saw and felt and experienced. Soon thereafter, I realized that God desired these words to be set to music…and it was so. That is why I shared earlier that the actual author of this song is the Lord God and I was but His instrument in relating this gift of love to me in this experience of Glory. The image of *Heaven and Earth* by Daniel Holeman is offered as a reflection of our hope of Glory. You are invited to transcend from fishing nets into the *shimmering of God's hope for us…*

Cast Your Net Again…For Such a Time as This (*From Grace to Glory*)

O Father, give the spirit power to climb to the Fountain of all light and be purified.
Break through the mists of earth, the weight of the clod, shine forth in splendor,
Thou that art calm weather and quiet resting place for faithful souls, To see Thee
Is the end and the beginning, Thou carriest us and Thou dost go before.
Thou art the journey and the journey's end.

(Boethius)

Heaven and Earth by Daniel Holeman

O Holy Vision Most Glorious
Words and Music by Lana Lee Marler, Arr. Basil Alter

Weary footfalls crowd the path, though burdened, pricked and smitten.
Drawn by hope, I reject the wrath; Sustained by promises written.

The eyes of my soul are lifting; My spirit is quickened as well.
Things too marvelous are gifting; The horizon revealing its tell.

O Holy Vision most glorious,
At last our eyes' longing behold
The shimmering of God's hope for us,
As the gold streets of heaven unfold.

The path is like the river of God, flowing smooth, glistening and pure;
Heavenly hues of understanding broad, Love's intimate Presence sure.

Swept into Light everlasting; The questions of life, there are none.
Our God, Whose breath is all giving, Calls us to where all breaths are one.

O Holy Vision most glorious,
At last our eyes' longing behold
The shimmering of God's hope for us,
As the gold streets of heaven unfold; As the gold streets of heaven unfold.

Music Hyperlink
https://cast.jacobsladdercdc.org/home/o-holy-vision-most-glorious

Glory Reflections 20__

Glory Reflections 20__

Glory Reflections 20__

Glory Reflections 20__

Benediction

May none of God's wonderful works keep silence, night or morning

Bright stars, high mountains, the depths of the seas, Sources of rushing rivers:

May all these break into song as we sing to Father, Son and Holy Spirit.

May all the angels in heavens reply: Amen! Amen! Amen!

Power, praise, honor, eternal glory to God, the only Giver of grace.

Amen! Amen! Amen!

Third-century Egyptian doxology

Even so...

I will see you again, when we are both like golden clouds on the wind.

References

Forward

Hosmer, F.L., and Weatherhead, L., 1979 *A Private House of Prayer.* New York: Abingdon Press. [Forward p. xvii]

Preface

Etchells, R., 2008. *Just as I am.* London: SPCK, p. 122 Carden, J. and Saunders, C., 1976. *Morning, Noon and Night.* London: Church Missionary Society. [Preface p. xix]

Introduction

Birch, J., 2013. *I Enter This Day With Joy – A Prayer by John Birch.* [online] Godspacelight. Available at: <https://godspacelight.com/2013/10/26/i-ener-this-day-with-joy-a-prayer-by-john-birch/> [Introduction p. xxix]

Brooks, P., n.d. *Phillips Brooks Quotes.* [online] Quotefancy.com. Available at: <https://quotefancy.com/phillips-brooks-quotes> [Introduction p. xxiv]

Bunyan, J., Stachniewski. J., and Pacheco. A., 1998. *Grace Abounding With Other Autobiographies.* Oxford [England]: Oxford University Press. p. 274. [Introduction p. xxv]

Carthusian, G. and Etchells, R., 1994. *Just as I am.* London: SPCK, p. frontispiece. Carthusian, G., Colledge, E., and Walsh, J,. 1978. *The Ladder of Monks.* Garden City, NY: Doubleday. [Introduction p. xxiii]

Kanefksy, R., 2020. [online] Twitter.com Available at: <https://twitter.com/thislouis/status/1237923746775629824?lang=en> [Introduction p. xxiv]

Lewis, C., 1994. *The Collected Works of C.S. Lewis*. NewYork: Inspirational Press. [Introduction p. xxiii]

Thurman, H., 1971. *The Inward Journey*. Richmond, Ind.: Friends United Press. Thurman. H., 2011. *Howard Thurman - "What Do You Want Really"*. [online] Youtube. Available at: <https://youtube.com/watch?v=cUsG4B8VKqQ> [Introduction p. xxv]

Truth, S., 2003. *Book of Life*. London: X Press. [Introduction p. xxiii]

Chapter 1. Grace

Augustine. Grace Quotes. 2021. *Quotes by Augustine*. 2021. [online] Available at: <https://gracequotes.org/author-quote/augustine/> [Grace p. 3]

Barclay, W., 2021. *Top 30 Quotes of William Barclay famous quotes and sayings*. Inspiringquotes.us. [online] Inspiring Quotes. Available at: <https://www.insiringquotes.us/author/9264-william-barclay> [Grace p. 3]

Buechner, F., 1993. *Wishful Thinking*. [San Francisco, Calif.]: HarperSanFransisco. [Grace p. 5]

Graham, B., 1981. *Till Armageddon a Perspective on Suffering*. World Wide Publications. [Grace p. 3]

Morley, J., and Etchells. R., 2008. *Just as I am.* London: SPCK, p. 152. [Grace p. 3]

Newton, J., 1779. *Amazing Grace – Wikipedia*. [online] En. Wikipedia.org. Available at: <https://en.wikipedia.org/wiki/Amazing_Grace> [Grace p. 9]

Nouwen. H., 1982. *Making All Things New*. [place of publication not identified]: HarperCollins. [Grace p. 6]

Underhill, E., 1937. *The Spiritual Life*. London: Hodder & Stoughton. Job, R. and Shawchuck, N., 1988. *A Guide to Prayer*. Nashville, TN: Upper Room, p. 315. [Grace p. 7]

Chapter 2. Peace

Carmichael, A., 2008. *Prayer Quote of the Month – 17: 2008 (The Prayer Foundation)*. [online] Prayerfoundation.org. Available at: <https:www.prayerfoundation.org/prayerquotes/prayer_quote_of_the_month_017.htm> Etchells, R., 2008. *Just as I am. London:* SPCK, p. 32. [Peace p. 17]

Cornell, W., and Copper, W., 1889. *Wonderful Peace.* [online]. Library.timelesstruths.org. Available at: <https://library.timelesstruths.org/music/Wonderful_Peace/> [Peace p. 17]

Graham, B., 2008. *Wisdom For Each Day*. Nashville: Thomas Nelson. [Peace p. 17]

Job, R. and Shawchuck, N., 1988. *A Guide to Prayer*, Nashville, TN: Upper Room, p. 324. Nouwen, H., 1982. *Making All Things New*. [Place of publication not identified]: HarperCollins. [Peace p. 21]

Lewis, C., 1960. *Mere Christianity*. NewYork: Macmillan. [Peace p. 20]

Lowell, J., 2021. *James Russell Lowell – Wikipedia* [online] En. Wikipedia.org. Available at: <https://en.wikipedia.org/wiki/James_Russell_Lowell> Weatherhead, L., 1979. *A Private House of Prayer*. New York: Abingdon Press, p. 72. [Peace p. 21]

Marler, L., 2021. *A Quiet Room*. Memphis, Tenn. Etchells, R., 2008. *Just as I am.* London: SPCK, Weatherhead, L., 1985. *A Private House of Prayer*. New York: Abingdon Press, p. 176. [Peace p. 23]

McIlhagga, K., and Compston, K., 1992. *Encompassing Presence.* London: United Reformed Church in the United Kingdom p. 178. Echells, R., 2008. *Just as I am.* London: SPCK, p. 144. [Peace p.19]

Meyer, F. and Weatherhead, L., 1958. *A Private House of Prayer.* Nashville, TN: Abingdon Press. p. 161. [Peace p. 21]

Tennyson, A., n.d. *The Higher Pantheism by Alfred, Lord Tennyson – Poetry Foundation.* [online] Poetry Foundation. Available at: <https://www.poetryfoundation.org/poems/45323/the_higher_pantheism> Weatherhead, L., 1979. *A Private House of Prayer.* NewYork: Abingdon Press. p. 126. [Peace p. 17]

Thurman, H., 1999. *Meditations of the Heart.* [online] Goodreads.com. Available at: <https://www.goodreads.com/book/show/208175.Meditations_of_the_Heart> [Peace p. 17]

Whittier, J., 1872. *Dear Lord and Father of Mankind – Wikipedia.* [online] En. Wikipedia.org. Available at: <htttps://en.wikipedia.org/wiki/Dear_Lord_and_Father_of_Mankind> Weatherhead, L., 1979. *A Private House of Prayer.* New York: Abingdon Press. p. 72. [Peace p. 19]

Chapter 3. Provision

Andrewes, L., and Etchells, R., 1958. *Just as I am.* London: SPCK. p. 2. [Provision p. 31]

Appleseed, J., 2021. *The Johnny Appleseed Blessing.* [online] Quotefancy.com. Available at: <https://www.beliefnet.com/prayers/catholic/meals/the-johnny-appleseed-blessing.aspx> [Provision p. 33]

Etchells, R. and Norwich, J., 2008. *Just as I am.* London: SPCK, p. 28. [Provision p. 31]

Appleseed, J., 2021. *The Johnny Appleseed Blessing.* [online] Beliefnet.com Available at: <https://www.beliefnet.com/prayrtd/catholic/meals/the-johnny-appleseed-blessing.aspx> [Provision p. 33]

Leatham, E., 2021. *A Child's Grace.* [online] Hymnary.org. Available at: https://hymnary.org/text/thank_you_for_the_world_so_sweet> [Provision p. 33]

Lucado, M., 2021. *Max Lucado Quotes – BrainyQuote.* [online] BrainyQuote. Available at: <https://www.brainyquote.com/authors/max-lucado-quotes> [Provision p. 34]

Whittier, J., 2003. *The Eternal Goodness Poem by John Greenleaf Whittier – Poem Hunter.* [online] Poem Hunter. Available at: <https://www.poemhunter.com/poem/the-eternal-goodness/> [Provision p. 33]

Wiesel, E., 2021. *Elie Wiesel Quotes.* [online] Quotefancy.com. Available at: https://quotefancy.com/elie-wiesel-quotes> [Provision p. 33]

Chapter 4. Faith

Barth, K., 2008. *Fifty Prayers.* Louisville, Ky.: Westminster John Knox Press, p. 31. [Faith p. 45]

Brancusi, C., 2021. *Constantin Brancusi Quotes (Author of Constantin Brancusi).* [online] Goodreads.com. Available at: <https://www.goodreads.com/author/quotes/427859.Constantin_Brancusi> [Faith pp. 45 & 48]

Buechner, F., 1993. *Wishful Thinking.* [San Francisco, Calif.]: HarperSanFrancisco, p. 29. [Faith p. 45]

Chisholm, T., 1923. *Great Is Thy Faithfulness.* [online] Hymnary.org. Available at: <https://hymnary.org/text/great_is_thy_faithfulness_o_god_my_fathe> [Faith p. 47]

Etchells, R. and Canterbury, A., 2008. *Just as I am.* London: SPCK, p. 60. [Faith p. 45]

Gleason, J., 1978. *Growing Up To God.* Nasville: Abingdon Press, p. 33. Lake, F., 1966. *Clinical Theology.* London: Darton, Longman, & Todd. [Faith p. 49]

Graham, B., 2013. *Billy Graham.* Nashville, TN: B & H Pub., p. 21.[Faith pp. 45 & 47]

Lewis, C., 1960. *Mere Christianity.* New York: Simon & Shuster. [Faith p. 49]

Tubman, H., 2021. *Harriet Tubman.* [online] Available at: <https://www.harriet-tubman.org/>
Bradford, S., 1869. *Scenes in the Life of Harriet Tubman.* [Place of publication not identified]: [Publisher not identified]. [Faith p. 49]

Wesley, J., Job, R. and Shawchuck, N., 1983. *A Guide to Prayer.* Nashville, TN.: Upper Room, p. 368. [Faith p. 49]

Chapter 5. Love

A'vila, T., Zaleski, C. and Zaleski, P., 2006. *Prayer.* Boston: Houghton Mifflin. pp.178-79. [Love p. 61]

Barclay, W., 1956. *Top 25 Quotes by William Barclay (of 77) A-Z Quotes.* [online] A-Z Quotes. Available at: <https://www.azquotes./author/912-William_Barclay> [Love p. 61]

Etchells, R., 2008. *Just as I am.* London: SPCK. p. 58. [Love p. 64]

Etchells, R., and Norwich, J., 2008. *Just as I am.* London: SPCK. p. 46. [Love p. 61]

Mandrell, B., 1984. *Born to Die – Barbara Mandrell.* [online] SongLyrics.com. Available at: <https://www.songlyrics.com/barbara-mandrell/born-to-die-lyrics/> [Love p. 65]

Neuhaus, R., 2021. *Top 25 Quotes by Richard John Neuhaus. A-Z Quotes.* [online] A-Z Quotes. Available at: <https://www.azquotes.com/author/10752-Richard_John_Neuhaus> [Love p. 64]

Chapter 6. Mercy

Bunyan, J., 2017. *The Poetry of John Bunyan – Volume ll.* [Place of publication not identified]: Portable Poetry. [Mercy p. 75]

Etchells, R. and Langland, W., 2008. *Just as I am.* London: SPCK, p. 118. [Mercy p. 75]

Lee, D., 2021. mobile.twitter.com@DrRobertGLee. [Mercy p. 77]

Lemmel, H., 1922. *Turn Your Eyes Upon Jesus.* [online] Hymnary.org. Available at: <https://hymnary.org/text/o_soul_are_you_weary_and_troubled> [Mercy p. 81]

Luther, M., n.d. *Top 25 Quotes by Martin Luther (of 951) A-Z Quotes.* [online] A-Z Quotes. Available at: <https://www.azquotes.com/author/9142-Martin_Luther> Luther, M., 2012. *Commentary on Galatians.* Createspace Independent Publisher. [Mercy p. 75]

Meyer, F. and Weatherhead, L., 1958. *A Private House of Prayer.* New York: Abingdon Press. p. 80. [Mercy pp. 77 & 79]

Rothe, J., Weatherhead, L., and Wesley, J., 1979. *A Private House of Prayer.* New York: Abingdon Press. p. 62. [Mercy p. 77]

Smith, A., 2012. *Manna For The Journey.* Westbow Press. p. 53. [Mercy pp. 75 & 77]

Chapter 7. Obedience

Alwood, J., 1885. *Tune: The Unclouded Day.* [online] Hymnary.org. Available at: <https://hymnary.org/tune0_they_tell_me_of_a_home_far_alwood?extended=true> [Obedience p. 93]

A'vila, T., 2021. *Teresa of A'vila Quote.* [online] A-Z Quotes. Available at: <https://www.azquotes.com/quote/685941> [Obedience p. 93]

Barclay, W., 1956. *Top 25 Quotes by William Barclay (of 77) A-Z Quotes.* [online] A-Z Quotes. Available at: <https://www.azquotes.com/author/912-William Barclay> [Obedience p. 89]

Dawson, G. and Weatherhead, L., 1979. *A Private House of Prayer.* New York. Abingdon Press: p. 126. [Obedience p. 91]

Etchells, R. and More, S., 2008. *Just as I am.* London: SPCK, p. 116. Appleton, G. and More S., 1985. *The Oxford Book of Prayer.* Oxford: Oxford University Press. [Obedience p. 89]

King, Jr., D., 2021. *Martin Luther King Quotes.* [online] BrainyQuote. Available at: <https://www.brainyquote.com/quotes/martin_luther_king_jr_137105> [Obedience p. 89]

King, Jr., D., 1965. *17 Inspiring Martin Luther King Jr. Quotes.* [online] Biography. Available at: <https://www.biography.com/news/martin-luther-king-famous-quotes> [Obedience p. 91]

Lewis, C., 1952. *Mere Christianity.* New York: Harper Collins. p. 131. [Obedience p. 95]

Macdonald, G., Job, R, and Shawchuck, N., 1988. *A Guide to Prayer.* Nashville, Tenn: Upper Room, p. 325. Macdonald, G. and Hein, R., 2004. *Life Essential.* Vancouver: Regent College Pub. [Obedience p. 89]

Pounds, J., 1906. *The Way of the Cross Leads Home.* [online] Hymnary.org. Available at: <https://hymnary.org/text/i_must_needs_go_home_by_the_way_of_the_c> [Obedience p. 95]

Travancore, B. and Etchells, R., 2008. *Just as I am.* London: SPCK, pp. 114-115. [Obedience pp. 91 & 92]

Waligur, S., 2021. Facebook post. [Obedience p. 91]

Chapter 8. Hope

Buechner, F., 1993. *Wishful Thinking.* [San Francisco, Calif.]: HarperSanFranciso. p. 46. [Hope p. 107]

Francis, P., 2020. *7 Inspiring Quotes From Pope Francis to Ground Us in This Time of Uncertainty.* [online] Thriveglobal.com. Available at: <https://thriveglobal.com/stories/inspiring-quotes-from-pope-francis/> [Hope p. 105]

Gasztold, C., Godden, R. and Primrose, J., 1947. *Prayers From the Ark.* Gasztold, C. and Etchells, R., 2008. *Just as I am.* London: SPCK, p. 50. Marler, L. and Gasztold, C., 2021. *Prayer of the Goat.* Memphis. [Hope p. 109 & 111]

Hippo, S., n.d. *Saint Augustine Quotes – BrainyQuote.* [online] BrainyQuote. Available at: <https://www.brainyquote.com/authors/saint-augustine-quotes> [Hope p. 108]

Job, R. and Shawchuck, N., 1988. *A Guide to Prayer*, Nashville, TN: Upper Room, p. 339. Nouwen, H., 1986. *Reaching Out.* Garden City, N.Y.: Image Books. [Hope p. 107]

Jung, C., Zaleski, C. and Zaleski, P., 2006. *Prayer.* Boston: Houghton Mifflin, p. 122. [Hope p. 105]

King, Jr., D., 1963. *NPR Cookie Consent and Choices.* [online] Npr.org. Available at: <https://npr.org/2010/01/18/122701268/i-have-a-dream-speech-in-its-entirety> Wiesel, E., and Wiesel, M., 2013. *Night.* Farrar, Straus, and Giroux, p. 112. [Hope pp. 107-108]

King, Jr., D., 1963. *NPR Cookie Consent and Choices.* [online] Npr.org. Available at: <https://npr.org/2010/01/18/122701268/i-have-a-dream-in-its-entirety> [Hope p. 109]

Martin, C., 1905. *His Eye Is on the Sparrow.* [Hope p. 108]

Merton, T. and Etchells, R., 2008. *Just as I am.* London: SPCK. p. 4. [Hope p. 105]

Smith, A., 2012. *Manna For the Journey.* Westbow Press, p. 15. [Hope p. 109]

Chapter 9. Joy

Barth, K., 2021. *Karl Barth Quote.* [online] A-Z Quotes. Available at: <https://www.azquotes.com/quote/19586> [Joy p. 121]

Barth, K., 2008. *Fifty Prayers.* Louiseville, Ky.: Westminster John Knox Press, p. 29. [Joy p. 122]

Bonhoeffer, D., 1986. *Ethics.* New York: Macmillan Publishing Co. [Joy pp. 119 & 123]

Brancusi, S., Zaleski, C. and Zaleski, P., 2006. *Prayer.* Boston: Houghton Mifflin, p. 272. [Joy p. 119]

Camara, H. and Etchells, R., 2008. *Just as I am.* London: SPCK. P. 26 Camara, H., 1987. *Into Your Hands, Lord.* London: Darton, Longman, & Todd. [Joy p. 119]

Jones, R., 1944. *In Times Like These.* [online] Hymnary.org. Available at: <https://hymnary.org/text/in_times_like_these_you_need_a_savior> [Joy p. 122]

Smith, A., 2012. *Manna For The Journey.* Westbow Press. p. 71. [Joy p. 121]

Topping, F. and Etchells, R., 2008. *Just as I am.* London: SPCK. Topping, F. and Kelly, N., 1982. *Lord of Life.* Lutterworth Press. [Joy p. 119]

Wesley, C., 1738. *And Can It Be, That I Should Gain?* [online] Hymnary.org. Available at: <https://hymnary.org/text/and_can_it_be_that_i_should_gain> Marler, L., 2021. *Amazing Love...How Can It Be.* Memphis. [Joy p. 125]

Chapter 10. Glory

A'vila, S., n.d. *A Quote by Teresa of A'vila* [online] Goodreads.com. Available at: <https://www.goodreads.com/quotes/66880-christ-has-no-body-now-but-your-no-hands-no> A'vila, S., n.d. *Saint Teresa of A'vila Biography, Facts, Prayer, Feast Day, & Works.* [online] Encyclopedia Britannica. Available at: <https://britannica.com/biography/Saint-Teresa-of-Avila> [Glory p. 138]

Barclay, W., n.d. *Quotes by William Barclay.* [online] GraceQuotes. Available at: <https://gracequotes.org/author-quote/william-barclay/> Barclay, W., 2017. *The Gospel of John.* WLK.; Illustrated edition. [Glory p. 133]

Barth, K., 2008. *Fifty Prayers.* Louiseville, Ky.: Westminster John Knox Press. p. 55. [Glory p. 135]

Bede, V. and Etchells, R., 2008. *Just as I am.* London.: SPCK, p. 10. [Glory p. 133]

Boethius, A. and Etchells. 2008. *Just as I am.* London: SPCK, p. 2 Corrigan, D. and Waddell, H., 1976. *More Latin Lyrics.* London: Gollancz.[Glory p. 139]

Delbene, R., Montgomery, H., and Montgomery, M., 2005. *The Breath of Life.* Eugene, Or.:Wipf & Stock Publishers. [Glory p. 137]

Donne, J., and Appleton, G., 1985. *The Oxford Book of Prayer.* Oxford: Oxford University Press. Donne, J. and Etchells, R., 2008. *Just as I am.* London: SPCK. p. 171. [Glory p. 133]

Habershon, A., 1907. *Will the Circle Be Unbroken?* [Glory p. 137]

Hammarskjold, D., Sjoberg, L., Auden, W., Markings, and Etchells, R., 2008. *Just as I am.* London: SPCK. p 16. (Faber and Faber 1904). [Glory p. 133]

Hatch, E., 1878. *Breathe On Me, Breath of God.* [online] Hymnary.org. Available at: <https://hymnary.org/text/breath_on_me_breath_of_god> [Glory p. 137]

Luther, M., n.d. *Martin Luther Quote.* [online] A-Z Quotes. Available at: <https://wwwazquotes.com/quote/463043> Luther, M., Lull, T. and Russell, W., 2005. *Martin Luther's Basic Theological Writings.* [Glory p. 135]

Mackay, R. and Weatherhead, L., 1979. *A Private House of Prayer.* New York: Abingdon Press. p. 265. [Glory p. 136]

Quoist, M. and Etchells, R., 2008. *Just as I am.* London: SPCK. p. 94. Quiost, M., 1965. *Prayers of Life.* Dublin: Gill and Macmillan Ltd. [Glory p. 138]

Truth, S., n.d. *Sojourner Truth Quote.* [online] A-Z Quotes. Available at: <https://www.azquotes.com/quote/297564> Truth, S., 2020. *"I'm going home like a shooting star". Sojourner Truth and Motherhood.* [online] Amdigital.co.uk. Available at: <https://www.amdigital.co.uk/about/blog/item/sojourner-truth-I-am-not-going-to-die-i-m-going-home-like-a-shooting-star> [Glory p. 133]

Benediction

The Wind and The Lion. 1975. [film] Directed by J. Milus. La Calahorra, Granada, Andalucia, Spain: Columbia Pictures, MGM. Herb Jaffe. [Benediction p. 149]

Third-century Egyptian doxology and Etchells, R., 2008. *Just as I am.* London: SPCK. P. 126. Hamman, A., 1961. *Early Christian Prayers.* [Benediction p. 147]

Disclaimer
This disclaimer ("Disclaimer") sets forth the general guidelines, disclosures, and terms of your use of the "Cast Your Net again...For Such A Time As This" Book ("Book" or "Materials"). This Disclaimer is a legally binding agreement between you ("User", "you" or "your") and Lana Lee Marler ("Creator", "we", "us" or "our"). If you are entering into this agreement on behalf of a business or other legal entity, you represent that you have the authority to bind such entity to this agreement, in which case the terms "User", "you" or "your" shall refer to such entity. If you do not have such authority, or if you do not agree with the terms of this agreement, you must not accept this agreement and may not access and use the Materials. By accessing and using the Materials, you acknowledge that you have read, understood, and agree to be bound by the terms of this Disclaimer. You acknowledge that this Disclaimer is a contract between you and the Creator, even though it is electronic and is not physically signed by you, and it governs your use of the Materials. Representation: Any views or opinions represented in the Book belong solely to the content creators and do not represent those of people, institutions or organizations that the Creator or creators may or may not be associated with in professional or personal capacity, unless explicitly stated. Any views or opinions are not intended to malign any religion, ethnic group, club, organization, company, or individual. Content and Information: You may not modify, print or copy any part of the Materials. Inclusion of any part of the Materials in another work, whether in printed or electronic or another form or inclusion of any part of the Materials on another resource by embedding, framing or otherwise without the express permission of the Creator is prohibited.

References Editor

Kathern Lynn Harless is an editor/writer of both fiction and non-fiction born in Oslo, Norway in 1969. Being raised in a military family, they moved every time her dad received his orders, hence her being born abroad. For the better part of 40 years Kathern has called Memphis home; she lives in the heart of Memphis, Normal Station Neighborhood, with her son Andrew and daughter Ellen, along with their Fox Hound pup Brandi. Ms. Harless' writing tends to lean towards the human condition. She has the uncanny ability to make your heart swell, shatter it to pieces, and melt the tiny shards with the stroke of her pen. In March of 2018, she made her literary debut as a contributing writer in *The Collection: Flash Fiction for Flash Memory* with the story *A Good Left Hook*.

For inquire information about Kathern Lynn Harless and her editing and writing services: (harlesseditingservices.com) and (https://medium.com/@kathernharless).

Artists

Featured Artist: Daniel Bonnell – *Cast Your Net* (Book Front Cover Art)*; Vortex of the Christ; Jesus Calms the Storm; The Right Hand of St. Francis; Pieta Meditation; Jesus the Boy; Mary Standing before Gabriel; Jesus Wept; The Father's Forgiveness; Glimpse of the Christ; Trinity and the Cross; Hope in the Heights; The Prodigal and the Father; The Road Home.*

My painting reflects on the ultimate human need to fulfill an intrinsic longing that extends from birth to death. Simply put, it is a need to be held. My art symbolically speaks to this notion, especially with darkness (black) embracing light (color), with negative space enclosing positive space, and with texture calling out to be touched. I paint primarily on grocery bag paper with mis-tinted house paint. In my process this surface is surrogate for human skin that reflects life, especially so, when the heavy paper is saturated with pigments, oils, wax, and fragrances. The concept of using something that was once a utilitarian container also speaks to the theme of being held. My latest paintings follow a path wherein they are recycled back into yet another painting, as is it were sacrificing itself for a greater work. The painting is never finished, it is only at rest. Such a process is known as kenosis, or purging of the essence within each painting to create a greater work of art. This process is born out of contemplative thought and writings of the mystics. Working on modest surfaces with humble means permits this direction in a very natural manner. My paintings become a creative conductor that allows me to be held.

Julie Hamilton – *Stairway to Heaven* (Book Back Cover Art)

Julie Hamilton is a freelance photographer seeking hidden and forgotten places along her travels. To view more of her work visit julie-hamilton.pixels.com. The image was captured during the summer along the little Sioux River in Iowa. The light was like a magnet, tempting me to walk further.

Sharon Freeman – *Yellow Orange Blue Watercolor Square design 3* (Title Page)

Raised in Longview, Washington, award-winning watercolorist, Sharon Freeman majored in fine art at Central Washington University. She studied watercolor with several nationally recognized artists and is an active member of the Southwest Washington Watercolor Society. Her art hangs in public building in Washington State. Sharon's ability to capture light and transparency sets her work apart from other watercolorists. She uses a limited palette with pure colors and layers thin washes (glazes) to achieve vibrant, glowing color.

Lori Pittenger – *This Little Light of Mine* (Chapter Title Pages Art)

I am a Pacific Northwest Artist, painting in oils to capture the beauty in life. My paintings are representational impressions of places and things that I have visited and viewed and am inspired to paint as an expression of feelings and thoughts these visual experiences provoke in me. With my background in Interior Design and studies in art, my aim is to create a sense of balance and harmony with a key focal point in the composition to achieve a pleasant and eye-catching piece of artwork for the viewer. It is equally important to me that there is a concept that adds depth of meaning to the work, which is often shared in writing about it when the painting is complete. My style is alla prima, painting for 2 to 3 days while the paint remains wet, and I paint directly to the canvas or panel without under drawing to keep my brush strokes and palette knife work free. My works are painted with colors that are true to the scene and nature; and with inspiration from many classical and some 21st century Impressionists as well, the oil paint is applied in a loose fashion that is impressionistic yet maintains a sense of realism. Often there is a combination of smooth, blended out paint, with thicker 'impasto' paint laid in at key areas of the painting. This helps draw the eye to focus areas and gives a tactile interest to the work. "My desire is to create art that inspires, captures a special moment, prompts thought, and brings joy to the lives of others"

Jelena Jovanovic - *Touch*

I am a freelance photographer based in Belgrade, Serbia. I began my professional photography career almost 15 years ago and since then my work has been published in numerous digital and print media worldwide. My photography interests range from commercial to artistic research. I feel photography gave me the possibility to mix art and creativity with the job I loves to do the most. I am a passionate traveler, explorer, dreamer and recently a mother.

Lori Wright Mackert – *Consider the Lilies*

This painting is credited to the Lord. Like all things I create, I felt it come from Him. I use an air gun rather than art brushes with the alcohol ink to create the ethereal background and flower shapes, and then add small amounts of detail with oil pastel. The entire painting is intuitive with no pre-planned outcome or expectation which is my favorite way to create.

Maria Hunt – *The Gift of Self and Spirit of Hope*

"Art, something I always wanted as part of my life, has become a passion that fills my soul, and leaves me full of joy, one brushstroke at a time." After 30 years as a successful business woman, my husband and I retired to the Palm Springs area, where I pursued her childhood dream of studying and creating art. I started in 2000 with art classes at College of the Desert, refining my skills in plein air painting by attending workshops across the U.S. My love for my Creator, and His creations, is evident in all my artwork. More recently, I used my talent to raise funds for various charities in the desert (Actual "Antique Pages" from my husband's grandfather's "Cyclopedias," printed in 1884, which provide the basis for participants to create their own works of art to take home and the class fee is contributed directly to the charity. (Go to Maria-Hunt.Pixels.com to see the art participants create in the "Art on Antique Pages gallery) Since 2013 I have donated a weekly, relaxing hour or so of fun to the mothers in crisis pregnancies at "Mama's House, for women avoiding abortions. (Go to https://www.themamashouse.org to learn more about their life-saving efforts. You can contact me at mariahunt@mindspring.com or, online at Maria-Hunt.Pixels.com to view my artwork.

Thomas Cheatham – *Heart and Hook*

I began photography as a 4-H project in grade school in Portland, Oregon, and have been hooked ever since. After I graduated from Northwestern University, my career as a television producer took me all over the world, to places I dreamed of as a boy. Now, I have embarked on a second career, in photography, and am still traveling in search of beautiful and meaningful images.

Daniel Holeman – *Heaven and Earth*

Artistic talent combined with life-long exploration of consciousness and devotion to self-realization has given me an ability to depict uplifting and profound sacred imagery. My inspirational paintings often have a strong impact on people. I feel it is not so much the beauty, but the place it stirs within that people are responding to. I invite the viewer to dive into a deeper dimension of consciousness while viewing my paintings, allowing the high frequency imagery to activate their own higher frequencies within. The imagery activates forgotten awareness of a felt-sense of HOME – a warm, familiar and heartfelt state of mind – and my videos are a deeply moving experience to behold. My primary role in life is that of a messenger and guide for all (who are ready) to realize our Unity. I offer insight, clarity and counsel on living in this world with that awareness. And the art that comes through me is the creative expression of that role. I am a way-shower, helping others to realize and live their unique higher purpose - their fullest potential, based on a foundation of Unity Consciousness, and the Clarity of Being who we are designed to be and the role we are here to fill in life. I am an Ambassador for the Gene Keys and Golden Path trans-
formation tools and offers introduction and guidance.
(www.AwakenVisions.com)

Featured Music Arranger

Hailed by the Memphis Commercial Appeal as a "teenage virtuoso," Basil Alter is a violinist from Memphis. Currently based in New York, he is a student at Manhattan School of Music studying violin. As a classical concert violinist, he has performed nationally and internationally to great acclaim. In addition, he is a featured performer on albums from a wide array of genres. Outside of performing, he is a sought-after music arranger and music transcriber for artists across the globe. He has been featured in the University of Memphis Magazine, WKNO FM's "Checking In on the Arts," and Jewish Scene Magazine. In the rare moments where he is not working on something musical he can be found doing the New York Times daily crossword. He is grateful to the author of *Cast Your Net Again* for inviting him and giving him the opportunity to complete the musical arrangements for her. Please visit his website: basilalter.com.

Contributing Music Arrangers

Jeremey Johnson, American composer and arranger, has been writing music in a variety of settings for more than fourteen years. He studied music at Ball State University followed by Indiana Wesleyan University. Including a degree in music education, Jeremey has a vast spectrum of experience from many genres that drives the creativity of his distinctly unique style, which has become a hallmark of new music in many circles. He is also a sought after clinician and conductor throughout the country. As owner and founder of High Note Music Industries, Jeremey provides of number of music services to both professionals and amateurs worldwide.

Robert T. Totten, classically-trained pianist/keyboardist, has been exercising his God-given gift since he was six years old. Robert grew-up in the church, playing gospel while in middle school, but by the time he started high school, it was jazz music which captivated his attention. He won Best Jazz Soloist in regional competitions in 2010, 2011 and 2018. His talent for spontaneity in providing keyboard arrangements on the fly are standard fare for this piano man. At present, Robert is a musician for the Navy Band Great Lakes, earning Flag Commendation Awards for performing music during and assisting 40,000+ recruits through quarantine operations during the pandemic. He has even shared the jazz stage alongside such greats as Chick Corea.

Sound Engineers

Music and Vocals recorded by John New Dollahite, Manager and Recording/Mix Engineer, at The Grove Recording Studio at Hope Church in Memphis, TN. Simple and honest with integrity, John has been crafting his skills in and out of the studio since 2001. Operating a home studio for a few years and now working in several different local studios, he has completed numerous full lengths, demos and EPs. He enjoys working with a variety of genres including folk, jazz, singer-songwriter, reggae, rock, country, world music, gospel and bluegrass. John captures authentic recordings… true to your sound.

Music edited, mixed, mastered and produced by Mark Polack - Engineer, Mixer, Bassist, Programmer, Mac Tech and songwriter based in Nashville, TN. He has worked with such greats as Kenny Loggins, Richard Marx, Paul Carrack (Squeeze, Mike & the Mechanics), John Oates (Hall & Oates), Steve Cropper, Anders Osborne, Tommy Sims (Bruce Springsteen, Bonnie Raitt, Sheryl Crow), Reggie Young (Elvis Presley, Waylon Jennings, Johnny Cash), Tom Petersson (Cheap Trick), Felix Cavaliere (The Rascals), producer Peter Collins (Rush, Elton John, Indigo Girls), Jewel, Lauren Hill and Kellie Pickler, to name a few.

Music

Amazing Grace
Lyrics by John Newton, Music: New Britain, arr. by Basil Alter; Scott Sturtevant - Piano; Vocal – Lana Lee Marler.

A Quiet Room
Lyrics by Leslie Weatherhead, Music by Lana Lee Marler, arr. by Jeremey Johnson; Scott Sturtevant – Piano; Jonah Murphy – Flute; Georgia Bourderionnet – Cello; Vocal – Lana Lee Marler

There is No I in You
Lyrics and Music by Lana Lee Marler, arr. by Jeremey Johnson
Scott Sturtevant – Piano; Georgia Bourderionnet – Cello; Vocal – Lana Lee Marler

Just
Lyrics by unknown author and Lana Lee Marler, Music by Lana Lee Marler, arr. by Basil Alter; Scott Sturtevant – Piano; Jonah Murphy – Flute; Basil Alter – Violin; Georgia Bourderionnet – Cello; Vocal – Lana Lee Marler

From Love…To Love
Lyrics and Music by Lana Lee Marler, arr. Basil Alter; Alyson Kanne – Harp; Adam Alter – Penny Whistle; Basil Alter – Violin and Viola; Georgia Bourderionnet – Cello; Logan May – Bass; Vocal – Lana Lee Marler

His Face
Lyrics by Helen H. Lemmel and Lana Lee Marler, Music by Lana Lee Marler, arr. Basil Alter; Andres Ayola – Oboe; Alyson Kanne – Harp; Scott Sturtevant – Piano; Basil Alter – Violin and Viola; Georgia Bourderionnet – Cello; Logan May – Bass; Vocal – Lana Lee Marler

Jesus Said
Lyrics from New Testament Gospels Matthew and John and adapted by Lana Lee Marler, Music by Lana Lee Marler, arr. Robert Totten; Scott Sturtevant – Piano; Vocal – Lana Lee Marler

Prayer of the Goat
Lyrics adapted by Lana Lee Marler from poem by Carmen Bernos de Gasztold, Music: Ebenezer Tune composed by Thomas John Williams, arr. Basil Alter; Scott Sturtevant – Piano; Vocal – Lana Lee Marler

Amazing Love…How Can It Be?
Lyrics by Charles Wesley, adapted Lyrics and Music by Lana Lee Marler, arr. Basil Alter; Scott Sturtevant – Piano; Vocal – Lana Lee Marler

O Holy Vision Most Glorious
Lyrics and Music by Lana Lee Marler, arr. Basil Alter; Scott Sturtevant – Piano; Basil Alter – Violin and Viola; Georgia Bourderionnet – Cello; Logan May – Bass; Vocal – Lana Lee Marler

Paradox
by Lana Lee Marler

It feels like nothing is new…

But God makes all things new.

It is the simple truth that it is not so simple.

If I could just get out of the way,

Then the way, my path, would open to me.

The Truth has never left…

It is right here if I just turn my head and believe I see.

Hence, the simple truth:

Believing is seeing

    And

        Seeing is believing…

            Turn your eyes upon Jesus.

About the Author

Lana Lee Marler offers her second book in this writing. Her first book, which was also a personal worship resource, entitled: Follow Me - A Seasonal Journey, was published in 2017. Lana is a poet, singer/song writer, and church music director. A wife and mother, she is partner in ministry with her husband who is a United Methodist minister. Lana is an artist in any medium, but long ago chose music to express her relationship to God. Her faith journey led her to a major in sacred music in college and has crossed the landscape of three denominations: Baptist, Methodist and Episcopal. Spending countless hours mastering the hymnody and liturgies of these quite varied traditions has added depth and richness to her Christian perspective. Moreover, her musical DNA is infused with the music of the times in which she grew-up – the 1960s. Whether the song is Joan Baez's "Swing Low" or "Just As I Am" sung from a back row Baptist pew, she connects with each tradition in authenticity. In 2004, Lana and her husband, Rev. William D. Marler, co-founded Jacob's LadderTM Community Development Corporation, a non-profit charity serving inner-city Memphis, where the Gospel of Christ is shared through community-building, housing rehabilitation and education. All proceeds from this book will go to benefit the communities served by Jacob's LadderTM. (jacobsladdercdc.org)

9781665712361